SECRETS OF A HAPPY HEART

Debi Pryde

Iron Sharpeneth Iron Publications

A Ministry of Ironwood

Newberry Springs, California

TITUS 2 SERIES

Titus 2:4-8

That they may teach the young women to be sober, to love their husbands, to love their children, to be discreet, chaste, keepers at home, good, obedient to their own husbands, that the word of God be not blasphemed. Young men likewise exhort to be sober minded. In all things showing thyself a pattern of good works: in doctrine *showing* uncorruptness, gravity, sincerity, sound speech, that cannot be condemned; that he that is of the contrary part may be ashamed, having no evil thing to say of you.

Copyright 2002 by Debi Pryde

ISBN 1-931787-05-0
LOC 2002105048

All rights reserved. No part of this book may be reproduced in any form or by any means, electronic or mechanical, or by any information storage and retrieval system, without written permission from the publisher. The only exception to this prohibition is "fair use" as defined by U.S. copyright law. All inquiries should be addressed to Iron Sharpeneth Iron Publications, 49191 Cherokee Road, Newberry Springs, CA 92365.

Unless otherwise noted, Scripture quotations are from the *King James Version*.

Managing Editor, Shannon B. Steuerwald
Photography and layout design, Susanna I. Capetz

Iron Sharpeneth Iron Publications
A Ministry of Ironwood
Newberry Springs, California

Table of Contents

LESSON ONE
The Secret of a Happy Heart 5

LESSON TWO
The Joy of Receiving God's Blessings 17

LESSON THREE
The Joy of a Meek and Quiet Spirit 25

LESSON FOUR
The Joy of God's Forgiveness 35

LESSON FIVE
The Joy of Forgiving Others 47

LESSON SIX
The Joy of Christian Womanhood - Part One 69

LESSON SEVEN
The Joy of Christian Womanhood - Part Two 75

LESSON EIGHT
The Joy of Overcoming Disappointments 87

LESSON NINE
The Joy of Overcoming Impossible Circumstances 101

LESSON TEN
The Joy of Understanding Anger 115

LESSON ELEVEN
The Joy of Conquering Anger 131

LESSON TWELVE
The Joy of Happy Thoughts 149

APPENDIX
Things That God Says Make Us Happy 165

Lesson Answers 171

Memory Verse Cards 175

Foreword

One of the early memories I have of my mom is of her sitting on the couch reading her Bible while my brother and I ran around the room playing hockey. I remember getting my small New Testament and sitting beside her, holding my hands just so, and wanting to read just like her. I grew up thinking all Christian kids had parents who were constant students of the Word of God. Ever since I can remember, my mom took the opportunity to apply Biblical principles to our lives, whether dealing with an angry neighbor who threw firecrackers at our dog, understanding why women wear makeup, or discussing the best way to keep kids from fighting in the car. Always, God's Word was exalted. The Bible study series is fun for me to read simply because the principles Mom talks about are ones we have discussed as a family over the years. After the Bible study books were first published, Mom told me she wrote them to continue to pass on the things she has learned—many of these truths have been a direct result of the influence of her parents and grandparents.

She once showed me a passage that I've grown to love. *Psalms 78:4-7* says, "We will not hide them from their children, showing to the generation to come the praises of the LORD, and His strength, and His wonderful works that He hath done. For He established a testimony in Jacob, and appointed a law in Israel, which He commanded our fathers, that they should make them known to their children: that the generations to come might know them, even the children which should be born; who should arise and declare them to their children that they might set their hope in God, and not forget the works of God, but keep His commandments."

My mother's example is a challenge for me to love God's Word in the same way, to seek the Lord for wisdom and discernment, and to rest confidently in His ability to guide me in His paths as I've been taught.

Michelle Brock

About the Author

Debi and her husband Tom have been active in local church ministries for over thirty years. For the past twenty-five years, Debi has taught and led various women's ministries including seminar speaking, college-level teaching, Sunday school classes, soul-winning and visitation classes, counseling, and Bible studies. Debi is a certified Biblical counselor through Institute of Biblical Counseling in San Diego, California.

Debi and Tom reside in San Dimas, California, and continue to be active in their local church through teaching and counseling. They have two married children who are also involved in local church ministries while preparing for further ministry.

How to Use This Book

Secrets of a Happy Heart is a 12-lesson study that includes a variety of helpful resources. With each lesson you will find two memory verses, discussion questions, practical exercises that provoke further study and meditation, wide columns for notes, insightful text that further explains Biblical principles, and verse cards that allow you to cut and carry the verses so memory work goes beyond the pages of this book. No matter whether this study is used for personal use or as a group Bible study, we trust that you will find Biblical instruction that will exhort you to live a happy, productive life for the Lord.

Lesson 1

The Secret of a Happy Heart

> Favor is deceitful, and beauty is vain: but a woman that feareth the LORD, she shall be praised.
>
> *Proverbs 31:30*

> The secret of the LORD is with them that fear Him.
>
> *Psalm 25:14a*

Key Thoughts

INTERNAL CHANGE
Results in a happy heart as you set your heart and mind on godly things.

EXTERNAL CHANGE
Results in temporary joy and a disappointed heart

Research Question: What can you learn about the fear of the Lord from the following passages?

Psalm 34:11

Proverbs 8:13

1. I choose to rejoice and be joyful in God because God has "clothed me with garments of _____ (*Isaiah 61:10*) and forgiven me."

2. When I choose to delight in God's _____, my heart is filled with joy. *Jeremiah 15:16*

3. I am happy when my heart is tender toward the Lord and I _____ (have respect for) the will of my Heavenly Father. *Proverbs 28:14; Proverbs 29:18*

4. It is not enough for me to _____ the commands of God. I am happy only when I _____ them. *John 13:17*

5. The things in the Bible were written for me so my _____ might be _____. *1 John 1:4*

To pursue happiness as a goal is wrong and is guaranteed to end in failure. Genuine contentment and happiness come only as a by-product of responsible living, as God defines responsible living. —Robert Needham

Being Happy

Feeling happy and being happy are two completely different matters. We can feel happy when our immediate circumstances please us, yet be a very unhappy person inside. In fact, it is possible to feel happy at the moment, while being in inward turmoil, with no peace or quiet contentment.

The Bible describes this human paradox in *Proverbs 14:13*. "Even in laughter the heart is sorrowful; and the end of that mirth is heaviness." Many people who are inwardly unhappy can laugh and cover up their unhappy hearts when they are around other people. When they are alone with their thoughts, however, they are anything but happy.

False Happiness is temporary, surface happiness without inner joy, peace, or satisfaction; it ultimately results in disappointment, self-deception, sorrow, and restlessness. False happiness derives from the selfish pursuit of what we believe will satisfy us and is dependent on circumstances. False happiness results when we fail to distinguish the difference between receiving good things from the hand of God versus taking what we want on our own terms apart from God. We may get what we want by ignoring God, but we will not be truly happy or satisfied with the acquisition.

Genuine Happiness is characterized by inner peace, joy, satisfaction, contentment, and confidence in a loving, personal God. Happiness is a gift from God. It derives from God, not self, and is a by-product of living right, making deliberate day by day choices and acting on them. It does not depend on circumstances. (See *Ecclesiastes 5:19-20*.)

Genuine happiness provides inner joy and lasting contentment whether our immediate circumstances are exhilarating or disappointing. Occasional sadness is a part of life—but for those whose heart is truly happy, even sadness has its own kind of joy and peace.

The Bible describes this kind of joy in *Romans 14:17*. "For the kingdom of God is not meat and drink; but righteousness, and peace, and joy in the Holy Ghost." True joy is not found in external things or circumstances, but in the unseen spiritual interaction that takes place inside the human heart between the Lord Jesus Christ and His child. True joy and peace come from God, on God's terms, and cannot be enjoyed without repentance toward God and a humble submission to His work in our lives. God's peace and happiness always result in inner joy, and in quiet confidence and contentment. Dependence on self ends in sorrow. Dependence on Christ alone ends in joy.

NOTES

NOTES

Happiness by Change

When people feel unhappy, their first reaction to their discontentment is almost always to change something in an effort to feel better or dispel their unhappiness. Many of these changes are not wrong in themselves; however, when change is made for the wrong reason, it never results in satisfaction. People usually regret the changes.

Check the changes that might apply to you during unhappy times.

_____Overeating or indulging in rich or sweet foods

_____Changing hairstyle dramatically

_____Changing clothes drastically

_____Changing home decor

_____Buying new clothes, car, furniture, sports equipment, etc.

_____Shopping for whatever looks appealing

_____Purchasing items connected with a "higher" social status

Escaping from stressful environment by

_____Spending time with friends more than usual

_____Over-involving oneself with recreation or hobbies

_____Taking on more ministries or responsibilities than you are able to handle

_____Desiring a change in church or ministry

_____Changing location or jobs

_____Desiring a new home or drastic remodeling

_____Taking a job outside the home unnecessarily

_____Changing marriage partners

_____Finding new friends

_____Fantasizing about sexual relationships or forbidden activities

_____Sleeping, withdrawing from activity

Page 8

Genuine Happiness Follows Right Actions

People naturally seek happiness by changing something. Indeed, the desire to find happiness through change is not altogether wrong. However, genuine happiness is the result of making godly changes in our hearts, not in simply changing our environment. Our lives are supernaturally transformed only as we align our inward desires and beliefs with those of God. This may mean changing the way we view sinful behavior, or changing the way we respond to life's difficulties and circumstances. Aligning our thoughts to God's includes changing our perception of who God is and how He sovereignly works in our lives. We change when we learn to recognize the abundant evidence of God's love for us and when we grow in our capacity to rest confidently in His promises and ongoing work on our behalf. To experience genuine change for the better, our entire purpose for living must yield to God's until our delight is to live to please God rather than to please ourselves.

As our minds change and we conform our thinking to God's way of thinking, our attitudes and our entire life begin to reflect a wonderful transformation. It is only when our thoughts, desires, and beliefs spring from our confidence in God's Word, God's promises, and God's character, that we can see clearly enough to make wise changes in our outward life and circumstances. Sorrow, disillusionment, and disappointment usually follow decisions and changes that are made *first* on the basis of emotion and changeable feelings rather than on the basis of Biblical principle. Our feelings, though God-given and helpful, were never intended by God to be the basis of decisions and changes we make in our life. God's intent is that we engage in a deductive and objective process of intelligent thinking that relies upon the principles found in God's Word. It is only as we develop the "mind of Christ" and view our decisions and potential changes in light of His revealed wisdom that we avoid the many deadly pitfalls of emotional decision-making.

A God-centered change of mind is always evidenced by our outward change in actions and responses. In *Romans 12:2*, Paul describes this process of change that takes place in every growing believer's life. "And be not conformed to this world: but be ye transformed by the renewing of your mind, that ye may prove what is that good, and acceptable, and perfect will of God." We become genuinely happy when we conform our minds to God's mind, when we grow in our knowledge of God, and of Jesus our Lord (*2 Peter 1:2*). To grow in knowledge, we must conquer those things that hinder us from acquiring the knowledge of God, for it is only as we know God that He opens our spiritual eyes to truth.

In *2 Corinthians 10:4-5*, Paul addresses the necessity of knowing God and conquering whatever hinders us from learning truth. He once again talks about the relationship between the way we think and the joy we experience in our Christian life. He says,

"For the weapons of our warfare are not carnal [worldly], but mighty through God to the pulling down of strong holds; casting down imaginations, and every high thing that exalteth itself against the knowledge of God, and bringing into captivity every thought to the obedience of Christ."

In summary, we have learned that real change (that results in a happy heart) does not first stem from an external change in circumstances or surroundings, but from an internal change of the mind and heart.

False Happiness Follows Wrong Actions

When the prodigal son in *Luke 15* decided to collect his inheritance and seek his happiness in the world, he longed for a change in his surroundings. No doubt he thought his home life was boring and unfulfilling. Perhaps he became convinced his father was too severe, stuffy, and restrictive. In any case, he likely believed his father was depriving him of pleasure that would bring him happiness and satisfaction. He was self-righteous and self-confident and thought he knew just what he needed in order to be happy.

In the process of time, the wayward son consumed all his money on senseless partying and spending until, as the Bible says, he *"came to himself."* The harsh realities of living to please himself brought him down into the depths of a sordid life. He began to have a change of mind about his father and the life of responsible living he had rejected. At some point, he acknowledged to himself how foolish he had been. He no longer saw his father as a harsh and restrictive ogre. Rather, he realized how good his father had been to him and began to recognize that his wise father had only wanted his good and happiness.

The once rebellious son developed a total change of mind about his father's character and his father's will for his life. His father's goodness and merciful character gave him hope that he would be forgiven and received. This change of mind resulted in a change of action. The prodigal now gladly repented and returned home to a loving father who was eager to receive him and restore happy fellowship.

The father in this story represents our loving Heavenly Father who wants the best for us and longs to bless us. Just as the prodigal had to change his mind about his father and acknowledge that he was not a cruel tyrant but a gracious, loving father, so we must change our mind about our good and loving Heavenly Father. We must willingly turn from living our own way and submit ourselves to Him. When we truly repent of our self-will, our self-confidence, and our efforts to seek our happiness outside His will, God our Father is ready and waiting to receive us and restore fellowship and blessings. Like the prodigal son, we must come to understand that our happiness is not the result of external changes, but internal changes deep in our heart.

Are Happy People Ever Sad?

The Bible tells us that sorrow and grief in times of loss are an inevitable part of life. They cannot be avoided or dismissed as evidence of an unhappy heart. To grieve or feel the painful emotions that accompany deep sorrow does not mean that we are unspiritual.

Even our Lord Jesus Christ experienced both the joys and sorrows of living in an imperfect, sinful world (*Isaiah 53:11; Matthew 26:37-44; Mark 14:34-42; Luke 22:42-44*). The Lord does not promise that sadness will never come into our lives. He does promise to comfort us in all our sorrows and to ultimately deliver us from sadness that comes as a result of loss or affliction. "Now our Lord Jesus Christ Himself, and God, even our Father, which hath loved us, and hath given [us] everlasting consolation and good hope through grace, comfort your hearts, and stablish you in every good word and work" (*2 Thessalonians 2:16-17*). Our great consolation is that Jesus promises to go through our dark valleys with us, and He promises to lead us once again into the sunshine. We have God's assurance that weeping may endure for a short time, but "joy comes in the morning" (*Psalm 30:5*).

As we turn to the Lord Jesus for strength and healing, we can be sure that He will, one day, heal our broken hearts (*Psalm 147:3*). Our happiness in difficult times, then, is not in having a supernatural ability to *ignore* emotional pain. Our happiness is a result of knowing how to successfully *overcome* emotional pain. Peace, in times of suffering, results from knowing and believing several important truths.

1. God will comfort our hearts in special ways as we turn to His Word.

2. God will not *waste* any trial we go through. He uses all things for our good and His glory.

3. God will, one day, completely deliver us from our present affliction, our tears, and our sadness if we will turn to Him in faith.

4. God is good and gracious and worthy to be trusted—even when we are perplexed, when we experience the pain that comes from being wronged by others, and when we lose something or someone dear to us.

Solomon made an interesting observation when he contrasted the sorrow of the godly with the shallow laughter of the lost in *Ecclesiastes 7:2-4*. He concludes that for the godly, sorrow has a long-term benefit; whereas, the cackling laughter of the foolish only blinds them to spiritual reality. Solomon tell us that "by sadness of the countenance the heart is made better"; whereas, those enveloped in senseless partying take no notice of evil, and perceive no pain or personal loss in judgment to come. Sorrow often puts life into clearer perspective and results in wiser choices that have eternal rewards.

While understanding brings tremendous light and joy into our lives, it also puts our sinful condition and the sinful condition of others into clear perspective as well. We must balance the reality of pain and sorrow with an understanding and an awareness of God's grace, mercy, and love towards us. Otherwise, the sorrows of life *will* steal our inner contentment and peace.

The Secret of a Happy Heart

Palm 25:14a says, "The secret of the Lord is with them that fear Him." In this verse the word *secret* implies an intimate relationship, knowledge, and understanding of God's ways. Such a relationship with God is not possible to those who do not fear Him.

Psalm 128:1a says, "Blessed [how happy] is every one that feareth the LORD." Only those who fear God will ever know Him in an intimate way, clearly discern His gracious will, and develop a truly happy heart.

Since the fear of the Lord and acquisition of God's wisdom are inseparable and crucial to our happiness in Christ, we must understand what it means to fear the Lord, and understand how that fear is connected with wisdom.

To fear the Lord means...

- We have a reverent regard for the importance and greatness of God.

- That reverent regard is tempered with a fear of the consequences of disobedience.

- In response to the above principles, we have a sense of thankfulness for the gracious mercy and love of God.

We develop a healthy fear of God when we become aware of God's presence and the reality that He sees and weighs all that we do and think. The Bible tells us that the fear of the Lord is to hate evil and arrogance (*Proverbs 8:13*). We learn to hate evil and arrogance when we realize sin's painful consequences.

The Bible says that, "By the fear of the Lord men depart from evil" (*Proverbs 16:6b*). The fear of the Lord is absolutely essential in order for us to overcome sin or experience the joy of the Lord. Christ does not spare us from the consequences of our sin. This reality makes us alert and eager to turn from sin. The ultimate result is motivation to live a responsible life (as God defines responsible), and to possess great joy.

God tells us that *both* wisdom and the fear of the Lord produce joy. *Psalm 111:10a* says, "The fear of the Lord is the beginning of wisdom." Only when we learn to fear God do we begin to acquire God's wisdom and understanding. Wisdom cannot be worked up by our human power; we must ask God for it and depend on Him to provide it as we study and obey His Word.

To be wise means...

- We have a God-given ability to comprehend and apply knowledge and truth to life's circumstances and problems.

- We respond to life's circumstances in a way that is consistent with Christ's responses.

- We understand that wisdom is the outcome of a healthy relationship to God Himself and cannot be separated from an intimate knowledge of the Word of God.

David said the Bible is what keeps us from the paths of the destroyer (*Psalm 17:4*). Jesus said the words of God are spirit and life (*John 6:63*). Peter said that through the knowledge of Jesus found in His Word we become like Christ and manifest His nature, the fruits of the Spirit (*2 Peter 1:2-4*). Wisdom only comes through *knowing and believing* the Bible! "For the Lord giveth wisdom; out of his mouth cometh knowledge and understanding" (*Proverbs 2:6*).

Why Do I *Need* Wisdom?

- To enjoy purpose and fulfillment in life - *Proverbs 4:7-8*

- To understand and apply God's Word - *Ecclesiastes 8:1*

- To enable to respond to life's problems successfully - *Matthew 7:24-27*
- To understand life from God's perspective - *Ecclesiastes 8:5; Proverbs 22:3*
- To prevent being deceived by sin or sinful people - *Proverbs 13:14-15; Proverbs 2:10-12*
- To enable parents to build a strong and godly home - *Proverbs 24:3*
- To enable leaders to govern effectively - *Proverbs 8:14-16*

Why Should I Desire Wisdom?

- To know the joy of God's love - *Psalm 107:43*
- To know the happiness that comes with wisdom - *Proverbs 3:13-35*
- To experience the joys of being blessed of God - *Proverbs 8:35-36*

How Do I Get Wisdom?

- Realize it cannot be earned, bought, or found anywhere - *Job 28:12-28*
- Realize it must be asked for, recognizing every gift comes from God - *James 1:5*
- Realize it must be *received* in humility; it cannot be acquired - *1 Chronicles 22:12; Proverbs 15:33; James 4:6*
- Realize that learning the fear of the Lord precedes learning wisdom - *Proverbs 9:10*
- Realize wisdom is learned through the process of hearing and responding obediently to God - *James 1:22-25; Matthew 7:24-27*
- Realize wisdom is the outcome of giving intense priority to seeking the Scriptures to know God - *Proverbs 2:2-6; Psalm 73:25-26*

How Do I Know God Is Giving Me Wisdom?

- When I hate sin because it is a grief to God and when I recognize and hate pride in my life - *Proverbs 8:13*

- When sin is something to be diligently avoided at its starting points - *Proverbs 14:16*

- When I have a desire to please and obey God - *Matthew 7:24*

- When I begin to understand and delight in the Word of God - *Proverbs 14:6*

- When I realize that my purpose is to be involved with giving the Gospel message to others - *Daniel 12:3*

- When it is a delight to be instructed and those who provide wise counsel are respected - *Proverbs 9:9; Proverbs 12:15*

- When listening to God is more important than listening to self or others - *Proverbs 18:15*

- When people's weaknesses do not arouse anger and contempt in my heart - *Proverbs 11:12*

- When correction is viewed as a blessing, not something to be avoided or hated - *Proverbs 17:10; Proverbs 10:8*

- When I do not harbor bitterness, resentment, or envy in my heart towards anyone and when my life begins to be characterized by gentleness and genuine love for others - *James 3:13-18*

- When it becomes important to me to speak graciously and be sensitive to others and when I understand it is a sin to hurt others with careless words - *James 1:25*

How Do I Keep Wisdom?

- By never imagining I can do a*nything* apart from God and never accepting praise for what God has given. We are always dependent on our God. - *Jeremiah 9:23-24*

- By maintaining a fellowship and relationship with God. Just as Samson's strength was dependent on his obedience with regard to his hair, the *secret* of our strength and wisdom is found in our maintaining dependence on God through a relationship with Him. - *John 15:5*

- By not assuming I am ever exempt from sin's temptations, or the chastisement of the Lord - *Proverbs 3:18; Deuteronomy 8:11-18*

- By daily searching out and pulling weeds of pride and self - *Proverbs 28:14; 1 Corinthians 10:12; 2 Peter 1:10*

NOTES

Things That Make Us Happy

Many events and experiences produce temporary happiness. These certainly are not bad in themselves. However, temporary elation is not the joy our hearts truly crave or the joy God wants to give. We need to first learn how to distinguish the difference between false and genuine happiness if we desire a truly happy heart. We must discern whether or not the source of our happiness is temporary or whether it will produce eternal joy.

As you learn to think differently about what makes you truly happy, you will discover true happiness beginning to grow. Use the exercise below to help you clarify your priorities and develop a Biblical view of happiness.

Circle *Y* for yes or *N* for no.

1. Would happiness in this thing be dependent on circumstances?
2. Would this give me temporary rather than permanent happiness?
3. Would this reflect my desire to please only myself rather than God?

		Question 1	Question 2	Question 3
1.	New clothes	Y N	Y N	Y N
2.	A better house	Y N	Y N	Y N
3.	Spiritual understanding	Y N	Y N	Y N
4.	More talent	Y N	Y N	Y N
5.	A successful career	Y N	Y N	Y N
6.	Popularity, more friends	Y N	Y N	Y N
7.	A perfect spouse	Y N	Y N	Y N
8.	Ability to live a disciplined life	Y N	Y N	Y N
9.	No problems	Y N	Y N	Y N
10.	More love for God	Y N	Y N	Y N

Lesson 2

THE JOY OF RECEIVING GOD'S BLESSINGS

Blessed be the Lord, who daily loadeth us with
benefits, even the God of our salvation.
Psalm 68:19

And all these blessings shall come on thee, and
overtake thee, if thou shalt hearken unto
the voice of the LORD thy God.
Deuteronomy 28:2

Key Thoughts

A Happy Heart
Understanding and obtaining the blessings that come from obedience and trust

An Empty Heart
Refusing to value God's blessings or submit to God's ways

Research Question: *Psalm 78:41* - "Limiting the Holy One of Israel" means:

Note: In the following verses the word *blessed* comes from the Hebrew word *esher* and means *how happy.*

1. How happy is the woman who refuses to participate with gossip and complainers, but instead _____ in God's law and _____. *Psalm 1:1-3*

2. How happy is the woman who _____ __ _____ and greatly delights in His commandments. *Psalm 112:1*

3. How happy is the woman who keeps_____ and seeks_____ with the_____ _____. *Psalm 119:2*

4. The woman who cares for her home and family and desires to live a godly life of faith is called *happy* by _____ _____. *Proverbs 31:28*

5. How happy is the women who makes _____ _____ her trust and does not need the help or approval of others who are prideful and deceitful. *Psalm 40:4*

6. *How happy* is the woman who has compassion on others in need and shares what she has! The Lord will take care of this woman when she is _____ _____. *Psalm 41:1-2*

To know the will of God is the greatest knowledge, to find the will of God is the greatest discovery, and to do the will of God is the greatest privilege. —Truett

God's Blessings are Wonderful!

God *is* concerned with our happiness! A spirit-filled life is described as a happy and blessed life, not a life of morose seriousness and endless suffering. When the Scriptures speak of God blessing His people, it often means to bestow happiness or prosperity upon them. God's blessings are *always* good and are always to be received with joy. Even the word *blessing* means, in part, *happy*. When the Scripture says, "Blessed is the man…" it is saying with enthusiasm and emphasis, "*How happy* is the man…" God blesses His children, not only for their good, but also for their joy. His blessings provide the means for us to live joyfully, even in this present world of trials and afflictions and sin. God wants each of us to know the joy of experiencing "the peace of God that passes all understanding" (*Philippians 4:7*) in the midst of trials. What's more, God grants the means for every single one of His children to obtain blessings and rewards that will last for all of eternity. We only obtain them, however, through faith and obedience to God.

The Deepest Longing and Need of our Heart

The rewards and blessings God desires to give those who love and trust Him are greater and more wonderful than anything we could ever imagine. He "is able to do exceeding abundantly above all that we ask or think" (*Ephesians 3:20*).

David said, "Many, O LORD my God, are thy wonderful works which Thou hast done, and Thy thoughts which are to usward: they cannot be reckoned up in order unto thee. If I would declare and speak of them, they are more than can be numbered" (*Psalm 40:5*).

We read in *1 Corinthians 2:9*, "But as it is written, Eye hath not seen, nor ear heard, neither have entered into the heart of man, the things which God hath prepared for them that love Him. "

One of God's sweetest blessings is the gift of wisdom. That blessing alone is more precious and valuable then all the money in the world. In Proverbs God says, "Happy is the man that findeth wisdom and the man that getteth understanding. For the merchandise of it is better than the merchandise of silver, and the gain thereof than fine gold. She is more precious than rubies: and all the things thou canst desire are not to be compared unto her. Her ways are ways of pleasantness, and all her paths are peace" (*Proverbs 3:13-15,17*).

NOTES

Think of all the things in this life that you may desire. None of them will provide the joy and blessings you can receive from knowing and obeying God. Nothing but an active relationship with Christ Himself will satisfy the deepest longings of your heart. Nothing but a relationship with Christ will give you the blessings of God you so desire.

God's Blessings are Contingent Upon Our Obedience

Considering all the benefits and blessings of a close relationship with Christ, why aren't more Christians excited about walking with the Lord? Why aren't more people thrilled about the blessings of the Lord, or rejoicing enthusiastically that we are the special objects of God's love and favor? Why are so many believers discouraged with the promises of God? And why do so many quit when the trials and disappointments of life come, while others endure and overcome each sorrow with peace and joy? Why do some Christians humble themselves under the mighty hand of God, receive His correction and find the answers they need for their life, while others are convinced there is no help for them and no blessing for them?

One reason Christians lack joy in walking with the Lord is that many do not understand that while God is good and gracious to His children, many of His blessings and rewards are contingent upon our obedience to Him. It is not God's desire to withhold blessings. He, as any good father, is interested in our welfare and delights in our enjoyment of His good gifts (*1 Timothy 6:17*). Nevertheless, God does withhold many blessings because of our own sin, lack of faith, absence of spiritual growth, or unwillingness to separate ourselves from worldliness. Many blessings are withheld until we are willing to obtain them patiently through obedience.

> *One reason Christians lack joy in walking with the Lord is that many do not understand that while God is good and gracious to His children, many of His blessings and rewards are contingent upon our obedience to Him.*

In *Psalm 78*, God sums up the story of Israel's history of disobedience to Him. The Bible says the children of Israel limited what God could do for them. They actually forfeited the blessings that God wanted them to have because they would not believe that God was good. They would not trust and obey Him. They would not believe that God desired to reward them for their faith and confidence in Him.

Page 20

Instead, the Israelites complained and worried. They were angry at God's provisions and ungrateful for His miraculous care for them. They cared only about what they wanted, not about the better things God wanted for them. When they should have been depending on God for strength and deliverance during times of suffering, they were outraged. Instead of acknowledging they were sinners who did not deserve the least of God's mercies, they accused God of negligence.

They would not humble themselves before God, nor yield their stubborn will to Him. Yet in spite of their selfishness and wickedness, God was full of compassion for them. He forgave them and did not destroy them. Though He still loved them, preserved them, and guided them by His skillful hand, He could not give them the additional rewards and blessings that He desired for them.

Trials are Opportunities for Blessings

How many blessings do we forfeit because of our unbelief? When we stand before God to give an account of our lives, will we find we have made the same mistake Israel made? Will we hang our heads in shame and wish we had believed the Lord and endeavored to obey Him with all our heart and strength?

The people who came out of Egypt with Moses are dead. They have no chance to change their story. They have no more opportunities to live by faith and receive God's blessings. But our lives are not over. We can still repent of our disobedience and self-will. We can still learn to trust God and seek Him with all our hearts. Our trials are only opportunities for us to grow and learn. They are opportunities for us to believe without having to see, rather than having to see in order to believe.

Perhaps you believe you cannot obey God. Perhaps, like Israel, you have convinced yourself that your situation is different and your particular circumstances make it impossible for you to obey Christ. Don't believe such a lie, Christian! Paul tells us in *Romans 6:14* that sin "shall not have dominion over you: for you are not under the law, but under grace." The believer *can* obey, for God has freed us from the enslaving power of sin and given us the ability to obey Him if we desire it. The problem, then, isn't that we *cannot* obey—it is that we *will* not.

If you are struggling with yielding your will to God and obeying Him fully, go to Him in prayer. Confess your lack of desire as sin, and ask God to give you a desire to obey Him. "Gracious is the LORD, and righteous; yea, our God is merciful" (*Psalm*

NOTES

116:5). He will forgive, help, and bless you if you will only humble yourself before Him, acknowledge your sin, and receive His forgiveness.

Perhaps you desire God's blessings but wonder why you have not obtained the peace and joy that God has promised to His children. Ask the Holy Spirit to reveal to you the cause of your discontent and restless heart. Then diligently search the Scriptures to find the reasons for your lack of joy. It might be helpful to ask yourself these seven questions, provided you are willing to be extremely honest with yourself.

1. Do I love God?
And we know that all things work together for good to them that love God, to them who are the called according to His purpose. *Romans 8:28*

2. Do I obey God's commands?
Now therefore hearken, O Israel, unto the statutes and unto the judgments, which I teach you, *for to do them*, that ye may live, and go in and possess the land which the LORD God of your fathers giveth you. *Deuteronomy 4:1*

3. Am I walking uprightly?
For the LORD God is a sun and shield: the LORD will give grace and glory: no good thing will He withhold from them that walk uprightly. *Psalm 84:11*

4. Am I seeking God with all my heart?
And ye shall seek Me, and find Me, when ye shall search for Me with all your heart. *Jeremiah 29:13*

5. Is my purpose in life to please God?
And whatsoever we ask, we receive of Him, because we keep His commandments, and do those things that are pleasing in His sight. *1 John 3:22*

6. Do I regularly read and meditate on God's Word?
Blessed is the man that walketh not in the counsel of the ungodly, nor standeth in the way of sinners, nor sitteth in the seat of the scornful. But his delight is in the law of the LORD; and in His law doth he meditate day and night. And he shall be like a tree planted by the rivers of water, that bringeth forth his fruit in his season; his leaf also shall not wither; and whatsoever he doeth shall prosper. *Psalm 1:1-3*

This book of the law shall not depart out of thy mouth; but thou shalt meditate therein day and night, that thou mayest observe to do according to all that is written therein: for then thou shalt make thy way prosperous, and then thou shalt have good success. *Joshua 1:8*

7. *Am I willing to have blessings delayed and trust God for my future?*
For ye have need of patience, that, after ye have done the will of God, ye might receive the promise. *Hebrews 10:36*

For additional study and enrichment, read a book that lists promises found in the Scriptures, such as *All the Promises of the Bible* by Herbert Lockyear. Go through the promises, noting God's promise and the condition we must meet to receive that promise. For instance, *Proverbs 3:4-5* tells us to 1) trust God with all our heart; 2) refuse to lean on our own reasoning or understanding; and 3) acknowledge or seek God in all that we do. The promise, provided we do our part, is that God will direct our paths. Some promises are unconditional and are ours simply because we are God's children. Other promises are conditional, meaning we need to do our part by obeying God's explicit instructions.

Trust and Obey

When we walk with the Lord in the light of His Word,
What a glory He sheds on our way;
When we do His good will, He abides with us still
And with all who will trust and obey.

But we never can prove the delights of His love
Until all on the altar we lay;
For the favor He shows and the joy He bestows
Are for those who will trust and obey.

Trust and obey, for there's no other way,
To be happy in Jesus, but to trust and obey.

Written by John Sammis

Lesson 3

The Joy of a Meek and Quiet Spirit

But let it be the hidden man of the heart, in that which is not corruptible, even the ornament of a meek and quiet spirit, which is in the sight of God of great price.
1 Peter 3:4

But He giveth more grace. Wherefore He saith, God resisteth the proud, but giveth grace unto the humble.
James 4:6

Key Thoughts

A Clear Conscience and a Happy Heart
Comes from humility and a right relationship with God

A Fearful and Irritable Heart
Comes from disobedience, doubt, and unresolved guilt

Research Question: According to 1 Peter 3:4, what does it mean to have a meek and quiet spirit?
(See chapters 1 and 2)

1. All of God's _____ should be the joy of her _____. *Psalm 119:111*

2. None of God's commandments are _____. *1 John 5:3*

3. A Christian's heart is filled with joy when she _____ in God. *Psalm 28:7*

4. When we fail to confess and forsake our _____, we are miserable. But when we acknowledge our _____ and seek forgiveness, we are happy. *Psalm 32:1-3*

5. Jesus _____ so that His people could have His joy fulfilled in them. *John 15:9-11*

6. When a Christian makes _____ _____ her goal in life rather than searching for happiness, she becomes happy as a by-product. *Proverbs 16:20*

Nothing is so strong as gentleness, nothing so gentle as real strength. —Francis de Sales

Truths That Set Us Free

Who but a believer in Christ would understand that the way up is really down? In the Christian life, the way to be exalted is to be abased (*Matthew 23:12*), the way to get is to give (*Luke 6:38*), the way to lead is to follow (*1 Corinthians 11:1*), the way to fight is to love (*Matthew 5:44*), the way to gain is to lose (*Matthew 10:39*), the way to be honored is to serve (*Matthew 20:27*), the way to conquer the devil is to submit to God (*James 4:7*), the way to be great is to be small (*Matthew 18:4*), the way to be strong is to be weak (*2 Corinthians 12:10*), the way to be rich is to be poor (*2 Corinthians 6:10*), the way to be openly praised is to secretly pray (*Matthew 6:6*), the way to be first is to be last (*Mark 10:31*), and the way to conquer the fear of man is to love and fear God (*Luke 12:5*). These are but a few of the seemingly contradictory truths that are, in fact, God's truth—truth that sets us free from anything that would enslave us or rob us of God's blessings and joy (*John 8:21-33; 13:17*).

Unbelievers view such statements as illogical, oppressive, or even absurd. They have no desire to give up their own methods of "getting ahead" or their own ways of searching for self-fulfillment. To submit to God and govern their lives by principles such as these would require them to humble themselves and admit what mature believers already know, that apart from Christ we can do nothing. The pride of man finds such ideas silly, if not repulsive. Paul's declaration that "I know that in me (that is, in my flesh,) dwelleth no good thing" goes against the very core of supposed human self-respect (*Romans 7:18*). So would David's admission that "I am poor and needy," (*Psalm 86:1*) or Jacob's confession that "I am not worthy of the least of all the mercies, and of all the truth, which thou hast shewed unto thy servant" (*Genesis 32:10*). Even to refer to one's self as God's "servant" rubs against the grain of human pride.

Man has a difficult time agreeing with God because man, by nature, is a rebel who resists God's authority and reinterprets God's laws to suit his own view of himself and his own desires. The human heart is so prideful and so easily deceived that it twists even the Gospel message to conform to its own way of reasoning. To many, God's declared provision for salvation seems illogical and demeaning. Man seems content, instead, to cling to his own good works as hope for salvation. He becomes offended by the declaration that man can only be justified and forgiven by believing (*Acts 13:39*), or that we work the works of God when we believe (*John 6:28-29*).

The flesh does not want to see itself as helpless or weak or vile. Rather, human nature desperately wants to believe it deserves God's grace and mercy—that God saves people because there is something good in them that merits God's favor. The unbelieving fail to understand that Jesus came to save those who admit they are helpless sinners in need of a Savior, not those who exalt their own righteousness and assure themselves

NOTES

they are not as wicked as others.

God's ways have never been and never will be like man's ways. God's ways are so much wiser and so much higher than man's ways that there is an incalculable distance between the two. Like a child who won't give up a plastic toy for a thousand dollar check, we often blindly and tenaciously refuse to recognize that our own ways and desires are foolish. Is it any wonder, then, that human beings have a difficult time believing humility is the only door through which we may come to Christ and find true peace and joy? James reminds us that God resists (is opposed to) the proud, but gives grace (unmerited favor, ability, and desire to do God's will) only to the humble—only to those who are dependent on Christ rather than self (*James 4:6*).

Humility, which is a prerequisite to receiving God's grace, means one has a right estimation of himself and a right understanding of one's dependence on God and unworthiness in God's sight.

Without God's grace, we cannot be saved, for we are saved by grace through faith and that not of ourselves (*Ephesians 2:8-9*). Without God's grace we cannot understand the Scriptures, let alone obey them or please God in any way. Whether we acknowledge it or not, we are dependent upon God for every breath we take and for every move we make. Paul, in speaking to the sophisticated citizens of Athens informs them "…in Him [Jesus] we live, and move, and have our being" (*Acts 17:28*). Paul reminds those who have privileges, abilities, or desirable qualities that it is God who gives all of these things, and since God gives them through no merit of our own, there is absolutely nothing for anyone to boast about (*1 Corinthians 4:7*). Even Jesus, our Lord and Savior and example to follow declared, "I can of mine own self do nothing." "I seek not mine own will, but the will of him that sent me."

Humility, which is a prerequisite to receiving God's grace, means one has a right estimation of himself and a right understanding of one's dependence on God and unworthiness in God's sight. Humility always produces submission to God's divine will and always gives up its own perceived rights; it is connected to fearing God and giving Him the respect and honor and submission that is due Him. God has a divine order to receiving His grace and blessings. "By humility and the fear of the Lord are riches, and honour, and life." *Proverbs 22:4* is just one of many passages that instruct us to humble ourselves before God if we would have the joys that only God can give.

Charles Spurgeon, in a sermon on humility said, "When God intends to fill a soul with His spirit He first makes it empty; when He intends to enrich a soul He first makes it poor; when He intends to exalt a soul, He first makes it sensible of its own miseries, wants and nothingness. If any man tells me that he is humble, I know him to be profoundly proud. And if any man will not acknowledge this truth, that he is desperately inclined to self-exaltation, let him know that his denial of this truth is the best proof of it. If you and I empty ourselves, depend on it, God will fill us. Divine grace seeks out and fills a vacuum. Make a vacuum by humility, and God will fill that vacuum by His love. I believe every Christian has a choice between being humble and being humbled."

Moses was a great and influential man who was first emptied of self-reliance and stripped of all human worthiness and glory. Before he could become the great man of God he was, he had to first come to the place where he would depend upon God alone to enable him to do His will, rather than his title or privilege or talent. When at last Israel was ready to enter into the promised land, Moses reminds the people that it was by God's power and grace that they would possess the land and enjoy its wealth. He reminds them that God is graciously giving them the land for His own glory, not because they merited His favor. He warns them not to forget that it was by God's power they came out of Egypt and by God's love and grace that they were sustained in the wilderness. He warns them not to say to themselves, "My power and the might of mine hand hath gotten me this wealth." Instead he beseeches them to remember the "Lord thy God; for it is He that giveth thee power to get wealth, that He may establish His covenant which He sware unto thy fathers, as it is this day." (*Deuteronomy 8:11-20*) Moses understood that God's desire was to bless Israel, but Israel's joy and blessing required them to acknowledge their dependence upon and thankfulness to God for everything.

A woman who is content and satisfied is able to accept both herself and her circumstances with quiet confidence in God.

It should not surprise us that God said of Moses, "Now the man Moses was very meek, above all the men which were upon the face of the earth" (*Numbers 12:3*). Moses demonstrated great meekness, or humility, in his relationship to the Lord. We see Moses' meek and humble spirit by his submission, reverence, and dependence on God. He saw himself as nothing, and God as everything. He recognized the emptiness and worthlessness of human endeavors, plans, and ideas; and he embraced the eternal rewards of obedience to God instead (*Hebrews 11:24-26*). This dependence upon God and emptying of self enabled him to trust God confidently without anxiety or distress. David tells us that God made known to Moses His ways, while He showed only His acts to Israel (*Psalm 103:7*). Knowledge of God and of Jesus our Lord always produces grace and peace in our lives (*2 Peter 1:2*). But unless we humble ourselves and look to God to open our eyes of understanding, knowledge and peace will elude us just as it did the children of Israel (*Psalm 119:18,27*).

God describes the true beauty of a godly woman in *1 Peter 3:4*. He says, "But let it be the hidden man of the heart, in that which is not corruptible, even the ornament of a meek and quiet spirit, which is in the sight of God of great price." This is the description of one who, like Moses, is humble and dependent on God. Such humility leads to a quiet spirit, or an inner state of peace that stems from confidence in God and freedom from anxiety or worry. This is truly genuine contentment in the fullest sense of the word. A meek and quiet spirit, then, is synonymous with the "godliness with contentment" that Timothy speaks of in *1 Timothy 6:6*. Jeremiah Buroughs, an old Puritan preacher, describes contentment this way: "That sweet, inward, quiet, gracious frame of spirit, which freely submits to and delights in God's wise and fatherly disposal in every condition."

A woman who possesses a meek and quiet spirit has the inner joy of a happy, contented heart—a joy that is not dependent on circumstances or other people for its peace. A woman who is content and satisfied is able to accept both herself and her circumstances with quiet confidence in God. She is able to sweetly rest in God because her heart is free from the turmoil of anxiety, unconfessed sin, misplaced guilt, or doubts about God's love and purpose for her life.

No wonder Timothy concluded that godliness with contentment is great gain! He is *not* speaking of a form of godliness that consists of rules and obligations, minus an intimate relationship with God. Keeping rules without a relationship with God ultimately produces arrogance or rebellion in a person's life. Any attempt to have a relationship with God without conforming to genuine godliness *likewise* produces arrogance or rebellion. When Timothy speaks of godliness with contentment, he puts the two together. He understands that true godliness is a gift of God's grace and stems out of an intimate and right relationship with God.

Acceptance

A woman with a meek and quiet spirit may not have the answers to every question that perplexes her. She may not have developed the maturity of a seasoned believer. She may fail repeatedly just as David did and need to go to God for cleansing and forgiveness. Nevertheless, she has learned to accept herself where she is at the moment and accept the limitations and unchangeable features God has given her. She is content to learn and grow as God leads her through the joys and sorrows of her life. She has come to realize that it is by God's power and strength that she becomes like Christ for it is "God which worketh in you both to will and to do of his good pleasure" (*Philippians*

2:13). Most of all, she has come to understand and thoroughly believe that God loves her, forgives her, and knows what is best for her each step of the way. As a result, she is able to place her trust confidently in her Lord Who knows and understands the things she does not. She is free from worry and self-condemnation and can live each day in quiet dependence on Christ.

Trust and Surrender

It is significant that the meek and quiet spirit God describes as being of great price to Him is spoken of together in the same passage as His instruction to wives to be in submission to their husbands. To sweetly submit to the authority of a husband requires humility and trust in God. In *1 Peter 3:6* God gave the example of Sarah as a woman who was characterized by a meek and quiet spirit and by obedience to her husband.

Sarah was beautiful, yet strong-willed and, at times, unbelieving. She lost her temper, she circumvented God's plan for her, she became discouraged, and she doubted the surety of God's promises to her. However, there is never an occasion recorded where Sarah disobeyed her husband!

She humbly called Abraham "my lord" and willingly walked together with him through their wanderings in the desert and through all the trials of their lives. Sarah was a woman just like you or me. She struggled with her flesh, her need to grow in faith, and her temptations to sin. Over the years, however, she developed an inner grace and beauty that Peter gave as a pattern for *holy women* to copy throughout the ages.

Complete Confidence in God's Love

Sarah lived a holy life, not a sinless life. The meek and quiet spirit that she possessed was the result of what she had come to believe about God, and a result of the choices she made to live a holy life for God's glory. The more Sarah learned about God's love and faithfulness, the more she came to believe in and trust in God's love. The more she learned to rest in God's love, the happier and more content she became.

The more we examine the Scriptures and learn about God's love, the more we experience God's faithfulness to us on a daily basis.

Sarah's testimony is similar to ours. The more we examine the Scriptures and learn about God's love, the more we experience God's faithfulness to us on a daily basis. The more we come to understand, believe, and trust in God's love, the more we will delight in and rest in God's love. And the more we rest in God's love, the happier and more content we become. In Josh McDowell's book *Evidence For Joy* the author sums up this principle well when he says, "Evidence (provided in the Bible) about God provides the basis on which to believe in complete confidence that He cares and will meet our needs."

When we examine God's Word, we begin to learn of God's loving, merciful, just, and faithful character. When we not only understand how wonderful Christ is, but believe it as well, we are able to have complete confidence that He cares for us and will meet our every need. This confidence is the very foundation of the meek and quiet spirit, which is to God of great price.

Developing a Meek and Quiet Spirit

Because humility is such an important prerequisite to receiving God's grace and ability to live a life of faith, we need to consider its development a major daily priority. This will require us to recognize our utter dependence on Him for *everything*. It will require us to cultivate an attitude of thankfulness to Him for all His work in our life and for *all* His good and perfect gifts, including our ability to accomplish and excel in any area. Recognizing that our daily blessings and opportunities come from the hand of God keeps us from taking credit for what God gives to us or enables us to do. It also compels us to ask, "Lord how can I use these gifts and blessings for your glory and the furtherance of your kingdom?"

Important points to remember:

- Humility is seeing God and self as both really are.
- Humility is part of fearing the Lord – *Proverbs 3:7*
- Humility is part of wisdom – *Proverbs 11:2*
- Humility is more rewarding than pride (self-sufficiency, self exaltation) – *Proverbs 16:19*
- Humility leads to honor – *Proverbs 29:23*
- Humility is blessed by God – *Proverbs 22:4*
- Humility is a prerequisite to receiving God's grace (the unmerited favor of God; the ability and desire to do God's will) – *Proverbs 3:34*

Make a commitment to begin or maintain a regular devotion time with the Lord. Having a set time and place to have devotions, as well as a good Bible reading plan, will encourage you to develop consistency and maintain long term success. Ask your pastor or a disciplined Christian woman to help you develop a Bible reading plan you are able to manage. Ask a friend to check up on your efforts to be committed and to encourage you in your commitment. Remember, in developing a good habit of devotions, it is important to establish consistency before length of time spent. Start out with a brief time of reading and prayer and lengthen your devotion time as you become more regular.

My devotion time is _____.

My devotion place is _____.

My devotion plan is _____.

Find five Scripture verses that provide evidence that God loves you. Mark them in your Bible so they are easy to find when you need them.

1. _____
2. _____
3. _____
4. _____
5. _____

What fears keep you from experiencing a quiet inner peace? Find a Scripture verse that answers each of your fears. You can do this by looking up the words *fear* or *afraid* in the concordance of your Bible, in a *Strong's Concordance*, or a *Nave's Topical Bible*.

1. fear:
   verse:

2. fear:
   verse:

3. fear:
   verse:

4. fear:
   verse:

5. fear:
   verse:

NOTES

Lesson 4

The Joy of God's Forgiveness

He that covereth his sins shall not prosper: but whoso confesseth and forsaketh them shall have mercy. Happy is the man that feareth always: but he that hardeneth his heart shall fall into mischief.
Proverbs 28:13-14

If we confess our sins, He is faithful and just to forgive us our sins and to cleanse us from all unrighteousness. If we say that we have not sinned, we make Him a liar, and His Word is not in us.
1 John 1:9-10

Key Thoughts

A Wise and Happy Heart
Being willing to humbly and honestly acknowledge sin and turn from it makes us happy

A Deceived Heart
Not being willing to acknowledge sin and turn from it makes us prideful

---

Research Question: According to *Proverbs 28:14,* what does *confess and forsake* mean?

1. God's forgiveness, peace, and happiness were only experienced when David acknowledged _____ _____ to God and did not try to _____ _____. *Psalm 32:1-5*

2. When we sin against another, we are sinning against _____. *Psalm 51:4*

3. Joy and gladness are restored only after we are absolutely honest with God about our sin and God _____ _____ _____. *Psalm 51:6-9*

4. We need God's forgiveness and the joy of _____ _____ restored in order to be effective teachers or soul winners. *Psalm 51:14*

5. Our hearts are happy and we have a desire to _____ aloud when we have a clear conscience before God, and guilt is removed. *Psalm 51:14*

6. We can be very happy because God does not require penance, self-afflicted suffering or punishment in order to forgive us. He delights in and requires a _____ _____ and a _____ _____ (repentance). *Psalm 51:15-17*

The disease of an evil conscience is beyond the practice of all the physicians of all the countries of the world. –Gladston

Humility Is Required

One of the most common causes of a lack of joy in our life or inability to find contentment is a failure to learn the importance of acknowledging and confessing our sins on a regular basis. Such a failure causes Christians to become guilt ridden and utterly miserable. We often blame others or our circumstances for our misery rather than realize it is our lack of humility and failure to confess sin that is at the root of our unhappiness.

How wonderful, instead, to discover the tremendous relief and inner joy that comes with being absolutely truthful with God as we confess and forsake sin! It is *only* as we learn to confess our sins that we learn of God's great love and mercy in a real, life-changing way.

God does not require us to be perfect, (as if we could). He does command us to be humble and honest about our sin. We need to learn to see sin the way He sees sin. A Biblical definition of sin is any lack of conformity with, or transgression of God's law. Paul says in *Romans 3:23*, "For all have sinned and come short of the glory of God." Any falling short of conformity to God's reasonable and blessed standard of righteousness is sin.

Wonderful changes take place in our lives *only* when we see sin God's way, which leads to our confessing and forsaking sin. Then we receive the forgiveness God offers—forgiveness based on Christ's redemptive work. *Only* then do we understand the wonderful joy of being forgiven, not because we deserve to be, but because God loves us, is merciful, and is very eager to forgive all who are honestly repentant.

The more we recognize our sin and see God's grace and love in His eagerness to forgive us, the more we love the Lord Jesus and appreciate what He did for us at Calvary.

David understood the blessing of becoming aware of and confessing his sin to God. David knew first hand the Lord's forgiveness and guidance in his life. In *Psalm 139:23-24* he says, "Search me, O God, and know my heart: try me, and know my thoughts: And see if there be any wicked way in me, and lead me in the way everlasting."

The more we recognize our sin and see God's grace and love in His eagerness to forgive us, the more we love the Lord Jesus and appreciate what He did for us at Calvary. But when we try to minimize our sinful attitudes and actions, ignore them, or cover them up, we become irritable, fearful, and spiritually cold.

Honesty Is Required

There are many devoted, active Christian women who know the Bible and can quote many Scriptures, but do not possess a meek (humble, gentle, not harsh) and quiet (inner peace of heart, undisturbed mind) spirit. Most often, they have come to see themselves as being very righteous, and have not cultivated a habit of acknowledging and confessing their sins the moment they become aware of them. They confess as sin the things *they* see as sinful, but not the things *God* sees as sinful. They do not recognize their failures as arrogance or self-centeredness, and therefore, do not ask forgiveness for or turn away from specific sins.

Remember that God said, "The fear of the LORD is to hate evil: pride, and arrogance, and the evil way, and the froward [rebellious] mouth, do I hate" (*Proverbs 8:13*). Instead of turning from their sin to God, these women often go on in their misery and emptiness, resigning themselves to a joyless life, or living as emotional or spiritual cripples. One of the most common root causes of anxiety and fear in women is an underlying fear of judgment that develops as a result of refusing to confess and forsake sin. This is just one of the ways fear and pride are linked.

A Right Relationship With Others is Required

Over and over again Scriptures warn us that we are not right with God as long as we refuse to acknowledge and make right any wrong we've committed against another. If we cannot make a matter right, we must at least do what we can to right any misunderstanding that alienates us from our brothers and sisters in the Lord (*Matthew 5:23-24; 6:14-15*).

Just as we are grieved when our children exchange hateful and cutting words or are alienated from one another, so is our Heavenly Father grieved when His children do not love one another (*1 Thessalonians 5:19*). We tend to greatly underestimate how serious a matter it is to God when we bicker and fight between ourselves and then fail to acknowledge and right wrongs we have committed against a brother or sister in Christ. If our hearts have not yet become hardened through pride and repeated refusals to right wrongs, such fighting will leave us irritable and rob us of joy and a clear conscience.

When this happens, we ought to immediately ask ourselves if we are failing to make whatever efforts are necessary to resolve ill feelings that exist between another and ourself. If our sin alienates us from our brethren or from God, we *must* accept responsibility for it and quickly confess it. Our sin may be great, as was David's when he committed adultery with Bathsheba and murdered her husband. Or our sin may be small. The size of the offense is not what alienates us from God. It is our proud refusal to obey God in dealing openly with our sin.

There are many times in our lives when we must flee from temptations, just as Joseph fled from Potiphar's wife. However, it is never right to flee from accepting responsibility for our sin when we are guilty. Joseph was not guilty when he fled the house of Potiphar. He ran from temptation, *not* from accepting responsibility for his wrong.

In contrast, David made a different and deadly choice. He chose not to flee temptation with Bathsheba, but instead fled from accepting responsibility for indulging in immoral thoughts and behavior. Though he later regretted it, he did not immediately repent, but devised a method to cover the sin, put it from his memory, and flee from the humiliation of accepting responsibility for his sin.

David found, as do all genuine children of God, that there is no place to hide when we try to flee from God by refusing to deal with our sin. The Bible says, "Be sure your sin will find you out" (*Numbers 32:23b*). It may not be immediate, but eventually God *will* expose any pride and sin in our hearts that we refuse to confess and forsake.

"If we would judge ourselves," God warns, "we should not be judged" (*1 Corinthians 11:31*). In *Proverbs 28:13* God repeats, "He that covereth his sins shall not prosper: but whoso confesseth and forsaketh them shall have mercy. Happy is the man that feareth alway; but he that hardeneth his heart shall fall into mischief." Do not try to ignore or hide your sins against others! Your unbelief, disobedience, and pride will cost you dearly in this life, as well as in Heaven. Your confession ought to be as open as your sin was. Secret sins must be confessed to God alone. Sins that involved another must be confessed to that person alone. Sins that hurt many must be confessed to those affected.

What Does the Lord Require of You?

Those with cold, self-satisfied hearts will not humble themselves to admit specific sins or deal with them honestly. They wish to pretend to be close to God when in fact they are not. These foolish people are as deceptive as Ananias and Sapphira were!

They forsake their own mercy, for the Bible tells us that God resists the proud, but He gives grace to the humble (*I Peter 5:5b*). To walk sweetly with our God on a daily basis requires us to be honest with Him. We need to be willing to yield our own will to Him daily, willingly doing His will rather than our own.

Our flesh screams and runs from confession and repentance. However, if we will humble ourselves each day and Biblically deal with our sinful, prideful attitudes and right our wrongs, we will develop a freedom and joy that is unlike anything we have ever known before. There is nothing so sweet and uplifting as walking with God with a clear conscience. That clear conscience comes, not because we are perfect, but because we have been honest, humble, and are *forgiven*.

"He hath showed thee, O man, what is good; and what doth the Lord require of thee, but to do justly, and to love mercy, and to walk humbly with thy God" (*Micah 6:8*).

Help for a Guilty Conscience

- Ask God to show you what sins in your life are unresolved and unforgiven. Read *Lamentations 3:40-41*.

- Ask God to give you a heart willing to be completely honest. Read *Psalm 51*.

- Write down each sin that comes to your mind. Read *Isaiah 57:15*.

- If the sin involves someone you have wronged, or someone who believes you have wronged him, immediately seek his forgiveness. Next make any necessary restitution. Extend loving acts that demonstrate your sincere desire to please God and love others. Read *Luke 6:35-37; Psalm 34:14,18; and Colossians 3:13*.

- Go to the Lord in prayer and ask His forgiveness, thanking Him for the grace and humility He gave to help you make the wrong right, and thanking Him for His complete forgiveness. Read *1 John 1:9*.

- If the sin does not involve another person, admit to God you sinned willfully, ask God to help you hate the sin, ask God's forgiveness and thank Him for His forgiveness. Immediately do whatever is necessary and can be done to avoid any further temptation to repeat the sin.

- Replace any wrong behavior with its opposite right behavior. Read *Proverbs 28:13 and Psalm 32:5*.

The Joy of God's Forgiveness

Forgiveness is the Only Solution to Guilt!

No human forgives perfectly. Nevertheless, we are to model our forgiveness after God's example of forgiveness. God forgives perfectly and completely (*Ephesians 4:32 - Colossians 3:12-13*).

Forgiveness is

1. A judicial act - official in the courts of Heaven
2. Given when a sinner repents

When God Forgives

1. God declares that the guilt of the sin is removed.
2. The record of sin and guilt is removed.
3. God remembers our confessed sin against us no more. He does not hold our confessed sin against us.
4. The punishment that we deserve for our sin is no longer held to that believer's account.
5. God restores the fellowship between Him and us that was broken when we committed our sin.

When We Repent We Must

1. Recognize and admit the sin to ourselves.
2. Acknowledge our sin to God and ask for His forgiveness.
3. Admit the sin was willful. We sin because we like it and do not care that it offends God, or, because the sin has become a habit.
4. Ask God to help us hate the sin.
5. Acknowledge wrongs done to others. Ask their forgiveness. If necessary, make restitution for wrongs.

To Know Joy After Repentance

Awareness of our guilt and offense toward God *must* be balanced by an awareness of God's great love and willingness to completely and immediately forgive. Joy follows

NOTES

confession and repentance only when we learn to thank God for His mercy and forgiveness. We must be absolutely confident in the Scriptures that teach us how God forgives when we repent. Continued guilt is not due to an inability to *forgive ourselves*, but an inability or unwillingness to believe and accept God's complete forgiveness.

A good way to conclude confession of sin to God is to read Scriptures on God's love and forgiveness. Write the following verses on 3x5 cards and read them after prayer until you have them permanently stored in your memory. Remember, God's comfort *always* follows the hearing and believing of Scripture.

Psalm 32:1-5   *Psalm 103:8-12*   *Psalm 130:4*   *Hebrews 4:16*

Psalm 86:5, 15   *Psalm 119:89*   *Romans 8:1*   *1 John 1:9*

The Bible Test for True Repentance - 2 Corinthians 7:9-11

Verse 9

Now I rejoice, not that ye were made sorry, but that ye sorrowed to repentance; for ye were made sorry after a godly manner, that ye might receive damage by us in nothing.

Repentance is not just feeling sorry for something, but being sorry enough to turn away from the sin to God.

Verse 10

For godly sorrow worketh repentance to salvation not to be repented of; but the sorrow of the world worketh death.

There are two kinds of sorrow.

1. Worldly sorrow is painful regret. It focuses on our feelings and is self-condemning and frustrating to us.

2. Sorrow that is godly has primary concern for the good of others and the honor of God. It seeks to right wrongs and to change behavior. Most people will quickly admit that they are a sinner. Few ever admit they are a *helpless* sinner, unable to save or change their own heart.

Worldly sorrow simply admits a wrong. Godly sorrow recognizes the helpless condition sin brings and turns to God for forgiveness and cleansing.

Verse 11 a

For behold this selfsame thing, that ye sorrowed after a godly sort,

- *what carefulness it wrought in you* (diligence to do right)

- *yea, what clearing of yourselves* (clear conscience)

- *yea, what indignation* (moved with displeasure over sin)

-*yea, what fear* (fear and awareness of God)

-*yea, what vehement desire* (desire to do what is right and acceptable to God)

-*yea, what zeal* (eagerness to serve God)

-*yea, what revenge* (willingness to carry out restitution)

Scriptures to Study

- Sorrow of guilt and joy of forgiveness   *Psalm 32; Psalm 38; Psalm 42; Isaiah 38:15-17; Isaiah 55:6*
- Model of repentant prayer   *Jeremiah 3:4,12-14*
- How often to forgive   *Matthew 18:21-22*
- Our mercy is to be as God's mercy   *Matthew 18:23-35*
- God's willingness to forgive   *Psalm 32:5; Psalm 40:12-13,17; Psalm 41:4; Psalm 130:1-4; 1 John 1:9; 2:1-2*
- Repentant sinners   *Luke 18:13-14; Luke 7:37-48*
- Peace is in believing what Christ has done, not in what we do   *Romans 5:1*
- To spiritually prosper, we must confess and forsake our sin   *Proverbs 28:13; Psalm 34:4; Psalm 147:3; Isaiah 57:15; Daniel 10:12*
- God loves and requires humility before forgiveness   *Psalm 51*

Psalm 51 - A Model Prayer of Confession

Verse 1   *Have mercy upon me, O God, according to thy lovingkindness: according unto the multitude of thy tender mercies blot out my transgressions.*

We can come boldly to God's throne because He is merciful, loving, and kind. He never rejects, condemns, or forsakes His own—even if He must chastise us.

Verse 2   *Wash me thoroughly from mine iniquity, and cleanse me from my sin.*

Only God can cleanse us from sin, change our hearts, or affect our wills.

NOTES

Verse 3 — *For I acknowledge my transgressions: and my sin is ever before me.*

The repentance demonstrated in this statement is genuine—David is accepting full responsibility for the sin with no rationalizing, minimizing, or justifying.

Verse 4 — *Against thee, thee only, have I sinned, and done this evil in thy sight: that thou mightest be justified when thou speakest, and be clear when thou judgest.*

Sin is against God. It is an offense to God because it violates His perfect law. Our willingness to sin proves the sinfulness of our heart in contrast to the righteousness of God's.

Verse 5 — *Behold, I was shapen in iniquity, and in sin did my mother conceive me.*

Sin is a part of our very nature from the moment we are conceived—we sin because we are sinners.

Verse 6 — *Behold, thou desirest truth in the inward parts: and in the hidden part thou shalt make me to know wisdom.*

God desires our absolute honesty with ourselves and with Him concerning our sin. Until we hate our sin, we will not have godly wisdom.

Verse 7 — *Purge me with hyssop, and I shall be clean: wash me, and I shall be whiter than snow.*

David's request reveals his humble recognition that only God can cleanse a heart from the guilt of sin.

Verse 8 — *Make me to hear joy and gladness; that the bones which thou hast broken may rejoice.*

When we refuse to repent, God will pursue and chastise us.

Verse 10 — *Create in me a clean heart, O God; and renew a right spirit within me.*

The word translated *create* means "to create out of nothing." David recognizes there is no good thing in Him—but that God must create out of nothing true righteousness of heart.

Verse 11 — *Cast me not away from thy presence; and take not thy holy spirit from me.*

Sin interferes with our fellowship with God.

Verse 12 — *Restore unto me the joy of thy salvation; and uphold me with thy free spirit.*

Sin destroys joy, but accepting God's forgiveness leads to joy's restoration.

Verse 13 — *Then will I teach transgressors thy ways; and sinners shall be converted unto thee.*

Only forgiven sinners are able to help others find reconciliation with God.

Verse 14 — *Deliver me from bloodguiltiness, O God, thou God of my salvation and my tongue shall sing aloud of thy righteousness.*

Guilt destroys peace—the removal of guilt brings joy.

Verse 15 — *O Lord, open thou my lips; and my mouth shall shew forth thy praise.*

The realization of God's grace and forgiveness causes those who are forgiven to be thankful.

Verse 16 — *For thou desirest not sacrifice; else would I give it: thou delightest not in burnt offering.*

Penance, doing good works, is not repentance. Good works do not absolve from sin. God does not want acts of worship while there is unconfessed sin in our lives. Penance centers and depends on what man does; repentance recognizes man's helplessness and depends only on what Christ has done on the cross on man's behalf.

Verse 17 — *The sacrifices of God are a broken spirit: a broken and a contrite heart, O God, thou wilt not despise.*

Before we can offer our love and worship to God, we must genuinely repent—this is what pleases God.

Verse 19 *Then shalt thou be pleased with the sacrifices of righteousness, with burnt offering and whole burnt offering: then shall they offer bullocks upon thine altar.*

Our good works and worship are accepted and blessed after repentance and confession.

Lesson 5

The Joy of Forgiving Others

And be ye kind one to another, tenderhearted, forgiving one
another, even as God for Christ's sake hath forgiven you.
Ephesians 4:32

The discretion of a man deferreth his anger; and it is his glory
to pass over a transgression.
Proverbs 19:11

Key THOUGHTS

A Joyful Heart Free From Bitterness
Equals forgiving the way God wants me to forgive

A Bitter Heart Full of Anger
Equals refusing to forgive, inviting severe consequences to my soul

---

Research Question: According to *Ephesians 4:32*, what does "even as God for Christ's sake hath forgiven you" mean?

1. When I choose not to be _____ about a brother's sin (transgression) and instead _____ _____ _____, I am happy. *Proverbs 19:11*

2. When I am able to meet a need to someone who hates me, and I meet that need, the Lord promises to _____ me. *Romans 12:20-21*

3. I can rejoice even when I am wronged and my offender does not repent because the Lord promises He will _____ me. *Psalm 5:11; Matthew 5:11-12*

4. When I regard offenses and suffering like Jesus did, I can be _____ with exceeding _____. *1 Peter 4:13*

5. It is _____ and _____ when Christians live together in _____. *Psalm 133:1*

6. Despising my neighbor will make me miserable; but showing _____ will make me happy. *Proverbs 14:21*

He who does not forgive others burns before him the bridge to God's forgiveness. —W. B. Knight

Forgiving Others Brings Joy

Forgiveness is Absolutely Necessary

Practicing Biblical forgiveness is foundational to a peaceful and happy marriage, home, and church life. The act of openly asking for forgiveness and graciously forgiving has the following effect.

- Keeps us humble and unselfish
- Promotes intimacy among family members
- Provides the right atmosphere for developing tolerance and understanding between family members
- Promotes a loving, safe haven for growth and acceptance
- Provides divine healing which is available in no other context

Joy is Linked to Forgiving Others

No joy is as sweet as the joy of having an intimate, loving relationship with the Lord and with other believers. Knowing the Lord Jesus as our Savior constitutes a relationship, not a religion. Because of that, our fellowship with Him on a daily basis is the cornerstone of our Christian life. This joyful communion is interrupted when we sin against the Lord, and is restored when we humbly acknowledge and turn away from our sin.

In the little book of First John we learn that one of the greatest sins we can commit is an unwillingness to love or forgive a brother or sister in the Lord. The Bible clearly teaches that we cannot enjoy the Lord's fellowship if we harbor grudges toward others, oppress others, or refuse to forgive others (*Matthew 6:14-15*).

John gives the reason why he wrote First John when he wrote, "And these things write we unto you, that your joy may be full." (*1 John 1:4*). What are *these things* John speaks of? He tells us what *things* enable us to have joyful fellowship with the Lord Jesus and others in *1 John 2:4,7,9-11*. "He that saith, I know Him, and keepeth not His commandments, is a liar, and the truth is not in him. But whoso keepeth His word, in him verily is the love of God perfected: hereby know we that we are in Him. Brethren, I write no new commandment unto you, but an old commandment which ye had from the beginning. The old commandment is the word which ye have

NOTES

heard from the beginning. He that saith he is in the light, and hateth his brother, is in darkness even until now. He that loveth his brother abideth in the light, and there is none occasion of stumbling in him. But he that hateth his brother is in darkness, and walketh in darkness, and knoweth not whither he goeth, because that darkness hath blinded his eyes."

Again he warns us in *1 John 4:20-21*, "If a man say, I love God, and hateth his brother, he is a liar: for he that loveth not his brother whom he hath seen, how can he love God whom he hath not seen? And this commandment have we from Him that he who loveth God love his brother also."

The conclusion we must come to is very important. Genuine love for *all* our brethren is an evidence of salvation and the change of heart that accompanies salvation. To keep (observe, practice) God's commandment to love our brothers and sisters in Christ in order to enjoy happy fellowship with Him is imperative. We cannot love God without loving others, nor is it possible to be right with God unless we are as right (as is possible to be) with others.

Love Covers a Multitude of Sins

Little five-year-old Johnny accidentally bumped into Timmy as he walked by him in the school lunchroom. Timmy assumed Johnny bumped him on purpose so he clobbered Johnny with his lunch pail while simultaneously screaming, "Johnny hit me!" Johnny was outraged that Timmy would clobber him with a lunch pail and accuse him of hitting, so he pushed Timmy into a wall. Enter the teacher. She now attempts to referee the dispute.

All of us who have ever parented small children can knowingly smile at this scenario. We've seen it happen in our own homes on a daily basis. Children tend to assume the worst when they've been slighted because it's part of their childish, foolish nature. This childish behavior is a routine problem mommy will spend a great deal of time and patience working on.

Some children grow out of it while others are never made to learn how to cheerfully accept or overlook the inconsequential transgressions of others. The children who don't learn often grow up with a *victim* mentality. They have a way of always assuming people are out to hurt them intentionally. Sometimes they become hypersensitive to discussing disagreements of any kind and find it unbearable to humbly admit faults or receive correction.

Page 50

Some develop intolerance for the imperfections, immaturity, or transgressions of others. They become a typical, disgruntled church member who leaps from church to church, never satisfied, never content that they are being treated fairly. Often they pick fights with family members, church members, neighbors, and friends, and they rarely admit fault or stop to consider the misery they impose on others as well as themselves.

Though real offenses are few, overreacting leads to the chain reaction of even more misunderstandings, false accusations, and wounded spirits. Because it is so easy for us to behave this way, it is imperative that we guard against assumptions, overreacting, and unmerciful accusations when considering a wrong we have committed against someone, or believe has been committed against us. Before we assume someone has wronged us, we *must* carefully clarify the wrong committed in *Biblical terms*.

Can you clearly identify a *Biblical* transgression? Is it something the offender can correct or repent of? Is your motive to restore fellowship that the wrong is interfering with, or merely to vent your disdain and personal disagreement? Are you prompted to go to your offender to retaliate in some way because you believe you have been rejected? Is this the old "you hit me first, so I'll hit you back" response? Is it possible you're reading into the situation and the offenses are not there at all?

If we have a problem with someone, or believe they are in error, we must first be sure it is something that genuinely disrupts Christian fellowship and therefore *cannot* be overlooked. If there is no Scriptural basis for our concern, we would do well to forget it. Far too many Christians live their life stewing, criticizing, and condemning others whom they perceive to be in the wrong. They are like five-year-old children, shouting foolish accusations at one another because they believe themselves to be victims of intentional harm.

Participating in such pettiness is particularly dangerous. We are warned that accusations of this kind are a device of the devil (*2 Corinthians 2:11*). Disputes often arise from wickedness (*James 3:14-18*), not a godly desire to walk together in Christian humility and love. Satan himself is known as the accuser. He is an instigator of false accusations that cause divisions and destruction in the body of Christ.

Let us learn to recognize and flee from this wicked human weakness that Satan delights to exploit for his own purposes. If we are offended where there was no offense intended, or if we are angry without cause, the transgression that must be addressed is our own. Making an issue out of incidents, differences, and opinions that are not sinful is self-centered, petty, and wicked. Such a practice can literally destroy other believers, discourage them, or cause division. It leads to our own misery and unhappiness as well.

NOTES

When Do We Confront an Offense?

Though we may know Jesus as our Savior, we are still *all* sinners though we have been forgiven and redeemed. We also are *all* maturing children of the Lord who are learning, through God's strength, to overcome the power of sin in our lives. Meanwhile, we *will* transgress against one another. We *will* at times make errors in our assessments of one another. We *will* make mistakes and offend one another.

It's not a matter of *if* we transgress against others or others transgress against us. The Bible says it is *impossible* but that offenses will come. We need to learn how to deal with transgressions Biblically.

On one hand, we are to pass over the transgressions and imperfections of others just as God does us. Mothers often pass over many of the immature actions and childish infractions of her small children. David said, "If thou, LORD shouldest mark iniquities, O Lord, who shall stand?" (*Psalm 130:3*).

God requires obedience, but God also recognizes our frailty and is merciful. If we went around pointing out everyone's faults and sins, we would become oppressive and destructive to others.

On the other hand, when we willfully choose to disobey God and insist on our own way, God holds us responsible for our behavior. He does not overlook self-will and rebellion any more than a loving and attentive mother overlooks self-will and rebellion in her children. Until we repent and seek His forgiveness, God does not extend forgiveness for our rebellion. Fellowship with God is interrupted until we are willing to recognize our sin and deal with the sin Biblically.

In the same way, we are to overlook the immaturity and transgressions of others, yet we are to lovingly confront a person who has willfully sinned against us in such a way as to hinder Christian fellowship, dishonor God, or bring harm to himself.

When we must confront a problem, the motive is not to tell our brother how much he has hurt us, or to force our brother to admit fault, or to vent our anger. It is to restore the fellowship that the offense has interrupted.

For the sake of peace, we need to lovingly overlook many sins, mistakes, and offenses because love demands our patience and mercy in this way. The Bible speaks far more often about overlooking the sins of others than confronting the sins of others. However, there is a time when it is actually *harmful* to overlook the offenses of others. The Bible clearly teaches us that we are not to suffer (allow) sin on our neighbor (Leviticus 19:17), but are to go to him and attempt to reconcile our brother to ourselves and to the Lord.

When we must confront a problem, the motive is not to tell our brother how much he has hurt us, or to force our brother to admit fault, or to vent our anger. It is to restore the fellowship that the offense has interrupted. In determining when to confront and when to overlook, we must be concerned with what God is concerned with, and that is, broken fellowship with Himself or broken fellowship between brothers in Christ. If God enables us to forget an offense, it should probably be overlooked. If, however, we continue stewing over an offense, or can't forget it, then the matter needs to be addressed. Either we are sinning by continually dwelling upon it, or the offense is a matter that is causing real division and harm to the cause of Christ.

Offenses that interfere with a brother's relationship to God or harm relationships to fellow believers must be addressed. To refuse to deal with them is not merciful or kind because such offenses grieve the Holy Spirit, cause division, and destroy the love and unity God requires between Him and His children.

Raising the issue of offenses or to humbly accept responsibility for our own sin is not fun or easy. Disciplining our children when they sin is not pleasant. But when the offense will ultimately destroy our children, or our friend, or the fellowship God requires, we *must* choose to do the right thing on behalf of others.

We Are Commanded To Go

At times when we are wronged, the offense breaks down our ability to have a loving, right relationship. We are commanded by God to go to our offender in an attitude of humility and love, doing all we can to resolve the offense and be reconciled (*Luke 17:3-4; Matthew 18:15-17*).

When we make it known to our offender that we believe he has sinned against us, we give him an opportunity to either repent, or provide us with additional understanding that might change our mind about the offense. The additional information may help us see our own responsibility or error in the situation. We are to go to our offender to resolve an issue and tentatively inquire as to the possible offense we believe may be the problem. We are not to accuse, but to restore broken fellowship.

We cannot delay seeking reconciliation with those we have wronged or those who have wronged us. To delay for any reason is actually an act of direct disobedience to God and only deepens the wounds. What we are really saying is, "I'll obey you, Jesus, when *I* feel like it, when *I* am ready." This is not an act of faith or obedience at all; it is a self-centered attempt to maintain preeminence and control in the situation.

Defensively maintaining one's own cause and stubborn will instead of immediately and humbly seeking peace and confessing wrong is the fuel that feeds the fire of contention and wounded spirits. That is why the Lord said in *Proverbs 13:10a*, "Only by pride cometh contention." Can you imagine how distressing it would be if God waited to forgive us until he felt like it? Thankfully, the Lord Jesus is always willing and ready to extend merciful forgiveness. He never withholds reconciliation for He has no desire to see us suffer needlessly.

When we obey the commandment to seek reconciliation, we must go with a readiness to both accept responsibility for our own sins and also to forgive the offender for his. This is the loving method God wants us to use to resolve conflicts and grow together in our Christian walk.

Our offenses against one another are not to be swept under the carpet and smoothed over by time—this is the way the ungodly deal with offenses. The Bible clearly teaches that Christians are to deal with their offenses truthfully and openly. The Bible way requires humility, love, mercy, and patience. In short, it requires us to exercise the fruit of the Spirit, which is the result of our believing and doing God's will (*Galatians 5:22-23*).

Before We Go

If we desire God's blessing on our efforts to resolve a conflict, we must be willing to go about it God's way rather than our own. Before we set out to deal with any offense, we need to be certain we are first and foremost obeying basic Biblical principles. We are not ready to confront a brother or sister in Christ until we have prayerfully and honestly examined own heart and have identified our own weaknesses and failures (being mortal, we all have them). God tells us, "And why beholdest thou the mote that is in thy brother's eye, but considerest not the beam that is in thine own eye? Or how wilt thou say to thy brother, Let me pull out the mote out of thine eye; and, behold, a beam is in thine own eye? Thou hypocrite, first cast out the beam out of thine own eye; and then shalt thou see clearly to cast out the mote out of thy brother's eye" (*Matthew 7:3-5*).

Are we willing to accept responsibility for our own sinful behavior apart from another's? Are we willing to recognize that our own perception of the problem may be wrong or inadequate? Do we readily acknowledge that our own heart is equally sinful and prone to being self-deceived just as others (*Jeremiah 17:9*)? An unwillingness to examine our own self honestly and humbly reveals a spirit of proud self-centeredness. Such pride will encourage those we confront to react with defensiveness rather than repentance. Neither God nor man despises the humble, but both God and man resist the proud.

When someone mistreats us, we all have a tendency to react with anger in some form such as bitterness or malice or resentment. Regardless of how we may have been mistreated, we have no justification for a sinful response. Unwillingness to acknowledge our own responsibility or wrong response hinders any godly resolution to a conflict or wrong committed by another.

In *Isaiah 58:9*, God makes it clear that He does not extend His blessing or peace to those who delight in pointing fingers at others' sins and failures with the intent to destroy, oppress, or embarrass them. God hates it when we speak pridefully in self-interest, or oppress others—even if they are wrong and need to be confronted. He calls it wicked to point out others' sins in an effort to elevate oneself or to gain esteem in the eyes of others. God warns that He will judge us and correct us if we persist unrepentant in this kind of destructive, unmerciful behavior.

It may be necessary and right to honestly confront another in love and kindness, but it is never right to confront anyone in an attitude of pride and condemnation. This is why it is so important to consider the log in our own eye and take care of it *before* we point out the speck of dust in our neighbor's eye. Perhaps the log in our eye is our pride or self-righteousness or improper reactions to another. Perhaps it is any number of wrong choices we made that contributed to the problem, or that grieved or provoked our neighbor. Whatever the log in our eye is, it needs to be taken care of *before* we approach our neighbors with their wrong.

Motivated by Obedience, Not Outcome

Most of the time, our interpersonal conflicts are quickly resolved when we approach them in a kind, humble way and speak the truth in love. We must obey God in dealing with others whether or not we believe our offender will repent or listen to our appeal. We must obey God whether or not the offender receives us well or responds as we had hoped.

God does not require us to change someone else's mind. We can only speak the truth humbly and lovingly. It is not our job to make others agree or understand. We are only required to address the error and their need to renew their mind through the power of God's Word (*Ephesians 4:15-25*).

God may use our willingness to appeal lovingly and honestly to our offender even after a long period of time passes. Perhaps our honesty, together with the honesty of others who confront him, will eventually cause him to see his error and avoid the consequences of his sin. Perhaps the Lord will use our loving confrontation, together with circumstances that He brings into our offender's life, to all work together to bring him to a place where he can acknowledge his wrong, repent, and be blessed of God because of his repentance.

However, even if our offender never chooses to repent or acknowledge his wrong, we still need to obey God and do what He instructs us to do. This obedience is important because, by obeying God in this way, we keep ourselves from feeling helpless or developing bitterness and resentment. Our happiness and clear conscience depend only on our obeying God and doing our part to resolve the conflict. It does *not* depend on whether the offender responds and repents.

Recognize God's Responsibility and Authority

If our offender does not repent or right the wrong after we have done all we can do to resolve the matter, we are to turn our case completely over to God. God will assume responsibility for dealing with the offense in His way and in His time. We are not to hate our offender, or in any way seek revenge, or harbor a grudge against him. God does not ever permit hating.

We must renounce anger or resentment against our offender. This means we are deliberately choosing to relinquish to God the full responsibility of dealing with the offense. (See *Romans 12:19* and *Hebrews 10:30*.) To refuse to do so is an act of extreme arrogance, for it says we do not believe God is willing and able to execute justice; and we want to reserve the right to punish our offender ourselves.

When we choose to harbor grudges, we are putting ourselves in the place of God, for God alone has the right and the ability to execute vengeance and justice. This proud and unmerciful spirit grieves the Lord and brings serious consequences into our lives. (Read *Matthew 18:21-35*.)

Granting of Forgiveness is Conditional

Christians often err by failing to differentiate between the two aspects, or parts, of forgiveness. Granting forgiveness is not the same as exercising a forgiving spirit or forgiving in our hearts. In *1 Peter 2*, Christians are instructed to pattern their reactions to suffering wrongfully after those of the Lord Jesus Christ. When He was mistreated, He did not swear and become angry. When He was falsely accused and berated, He did not berate and accuse in return. When He was physically abused, He did not hurl threats and promise revenge. Instead, Jesus immediately committed His case to God Who judges righteously. This is the same spirit of forgiveness that we are to exercise when we are mistreated, even when there is no apparent repentance on the part of an offender. It is a completely unnatural reaction that requires the supernatural work of God's Spirit in our hearts. The instructions given to us in *1 Peter 2* ought to provoke every Christian to cry, "Lord Jesus, increase my faith!" Nevertheless, when we forgive an unrepentant offender in this way, we are not granting him forgiveness or in any way implying that the sin should not be punished or dealt with appropriately by God or man.

When we grant our forgiveness, we are doing more than exercising a forgiving spirit and refusing to hold a grudge or exact revenge. We are restoring fellowship that was broken or damaged by the offense and are promising to treat an offender as though the offense never happened. We are saying that we will not hold the offense against the offender in any way or bring it up as an unresolved offense. Granting forgiveness does not mean trust is immediately restored nor does it mean a former position that has been forfeited can, or should, be restored. Granting forgiveness does not mean the consequences of the offense can be reversed, nor does it mean that the need for spiritual renewal and growth are no longer needed. The offending party may have problems that require extensive help to overcome before life can return to "normal." To grant forgiveness means that we will restore our friendship and provide Christian love and support, even when the offense has brought with it irreversible damage.

Forgiveness means fellowship with God has been restored completely and is present even when the painful consequences or correction of sin is being carried out.

The Scriptures teach that we are to pattern our forgiveness after God's forgiveness. *Colossians 3:13* reminds us "…even as Christ forgave you, so also do ye." When God forgives, He removes the guilt and punishment that the sin deserves and restores the fellowship that was broken by the commission of the sin. Though God forgives a sinner and brings him back into fellowship with Himself, He may use various means to produce a lasting change and correct one who has been overtaken in a fault. Yet this correction is

not punitive and is not the result of God distancing Himself from the one who has sinned. Forgiveness means fellowship with God has been restored completely and is present even when the painful consequences or correction of sin is being carried out.

God is *always* ready to forgive any who repent (or have a change of mind about the sin and willingly turn from it). Like our Heavenly Father, we must also be ready and willing to forgive others, no matter how they have sinned against others or us. Yet we must also recognize that there is a world of difference between being ready and willing in our heart to forgive any offense and actually *granting* forgiveness, just as there is a world of difference between God's readiness and willingness to forgive and His granting forgiveness.

In *Psalm 86:5* the Lord tells us "For thou, Lord, art good, and ready to forgive; and plenteous in mercy unto all them that call upon thee." Notice that God is ready to forgive, but there is a condition that must be met before He does forgive. This promise of forgiveness is only to those who call upon Him and seek His forgiveness.

In *1 John 1:9* we read, "*If* we confess our sins, He is faithful and just to forgive us our sins and to cleanse us from all unrighteousness." The word *if* means "conditional; provided that." When we willfully choose to disobey God and insist on our own way, God holds us responsible for our behavior until we confess and forsake the sin.

Luke 17:3 says, "Take heed to yourselves, *if* thy brother trespass against thee, rebuke him; and *if* he repent, forgive him. And *if* he trespass against thee seven times in a day, and seven times in a day turn again to thee saying, I repent, thou shalt forgive him." Remember, *if* means "conditional; provided that." Nowhere in the Bible are we taught that God grants forgiveness apart from the means He has provided for us (repentance). Nor does the Scripture teach that we are to *grant* forgiveness to an unrepentant person.

Nevertheless, we are to forgive in our hearts and be willing to grant complete forgiveness (restoration of fellowship) when they repent. We are not permitted to hold a grudge or harbor anger and bitterness against others even when they *are* unrepentant. And we are never permitted to carry out revenge.

Secular psychologists and Christian psychologists alike often teach a very unbiblical concept of forgiveness. Their approach is becoming increasingly accepted, even in Christian circles, to teach that one must unconditionally grant forgiveness to individuals, groups of people, dead relatives, imaginary people, animals, etc. in order to free oneself of guilt feelings and unhappiness caused by sins committed against us.

The idea of granting forgiveness without repentance is so widely accepted that believers and unbelievers alike quite easily assume they are forgiven and forgiving, when in fact they are not. Some people go so far as to believe Jesus died and paid for the sins of the whole world and consequently, the whole world is saved apart from individual faith and repentance toward Christ. Nowhere in the Bible are we taught that God grants forgiveness apart from our repentance.

Does Jesus Forgive Apart From Repentance?

The account of Jesus praying, "Father forgive them, for they know not what they do" (*Luke 23:34*) is commonly used to support the idea that Jesus grants forgiveness unconditionally. Some also point out the martyred Stephen's prayer, "Lord, lay not this sin to their charge" (*Acts 7:60b*). If Jesus and Stephen unconditionally granted forgiveness to those who murdered them, then that would mean they were forgiven apart from the hearing of the Gospel and receiving salvation.

The prayer Jesus (and Stephen) prayed was not a grant of forgiveness. It was a prayer expressing Christ's willingness to completely absolve those who were crucifying Him from the punishment of their sin. Such a dying request demonstrated a spirit of love and forgiveness in the face of unparallel suffering as opposed to a spirit of revenge and seething hatred. Jesus' and Stephen's statement was a petition for God's mercy that their persecutors might have the opportunity to repent of their deed and receive Christ's forgiveness. Christ did not desire retribution or vengeance on His abusers. He desired their repentance and reconciliation.

In answer to our Lord's prayer, many of those who crucified Him heard the Gospel preached by Peter at Pentecost, truly repented, and received forgiveness of their sins. The Scriptures remind us, "How then shall they call on Him in whom they have not believed? And how shall they hear without a preacher?" (*Romans 10:14*).

Likewise, Stephen's prayer was answered in that many who participated in his murder later heard the Gospel and received salvation and forgiveness of sins, including the apostle Paul. Jesus' and Stephen's dying words are wonderful illustrations of love that was willing to forgive even a sin so grievous as the torture and murder of their bodies.

When we pray for our offenders, do we, like Stephen, desire reconciliation and pray they will repent and be blessed? Or do we pray God will destroy them and inflict pain on them equal to the pain they have inflicted on us?

In *Matthew 5:23-24* we read, "Therefore if thou bring thy gift to the altar, and there rememberest that thy brother hath aught against thee; leave there thy gift before the altar, and go thy way; first be reconciled to thy brother, and then come and offer thy gift." In the next chapter our Lord again addresses the issue of reconciliation and says, "For if ye forgive men their trespasses, your heavenly Father will also forgive you: but if ye forgive not men their trespasses, neither will your Father forgive your trespasses" (*Matthew 6:14-15*).

This passage teaches that if we are unwilling to forgive in our hearts and reconcile (make things right) with a brother or sister, we cannot obtain forgiveness and reconciliation with the Father. An unwillingness to forgive does not sever our sonship, or salvation. An unforgiving spirit separates us from an intimate relationship with God which results in the hardening of our heart, misery, and, ultimately, the Father's discipline in our lives.

If you do not forgive in your heart, it will become impossible for you to fully love and enjoy the Lord or other believers. You cannot love your enemies, bless those who curse you, or pray for those who despitefully use you if you will not forgive. It will be impossible for you to love one whom you have not forgiven from your heart and with whom you are not willing to reconcile. If we are truly willing and ready to forgive the transgressions of others, there will also be a genuine desire to be reconciled to the brother or sister in Christ. This willingness and desire to forgive is what releases us from bitterness, anger, and resentment toward others who have hurt us.

When we are forgiving in our hearts and ready to grant forgiveness, we are saying that we will deal with the pain of the offense Scripturally. We are saying we will ***not*** respond to the mistreatment sinfully, but will deliberately choose not to hold it against the offender or bring it up to other people. We are saying we will not dwell on the mistreatment, but will do all we can to resolve it and then leave the offense with God. We are *not* implying the mistreatment wasn't *that bad* or wasn't *that sinful* or even intentional. We are merely choosing to deal with what really happened in a godly way, as Christ would have responded if the offense had happened to Him.

We must believe that we can forgive, because God says that we can through His strength the very moment that we will. It is not that we **cannot** forgive; it is that we **will not.** Forgiving is not easy. In fact, it is sometimes very difficult and costly. Just remember that Jesus' sufferings on the cross for us were not easy to bear. His sufferings were very costly.

We must also remember that it is 100% unnatural to forgive. In fact, it is impossible for non-Christians to forgive like Christ would. We must have God's redemptive grace in our own life before we can forgive anybody in this way.

A genuine willingness to forgive always results in the following:

- A willingness to bring the offense to our offender's attention so it can be resolved
- A willingness to release the offender from punishment the moment he repents
- A willingness to restore fellowship and treat the offender as though the offense never occurred.

If we are not willing to forgive from our hearts in this way, God will not restore fellowship with us until we do. If God intends for us to grant forgiveness unconditionally without going to our brother to be reconciled, He would not have carefully instructed us in numerous other Scriptures to go through the process of rebuking, repenting, and then forgiving where offenses have been committed.

Our place is not to punish or inflict hardship designed to make the repentant brother more sorrowful for the wrong done or to remind him of his sin.

The Bible clearly teaches there are conditions that must be met before forgiveness can be granted. Nevertheless, we *are* to forgive in our hearts and be ready and willing to grant forgiveness *always*.

We Are to Treat the Forgiven as Christ Treats Them

When we grant forgiveness to those who repent, thereby promising to restore fellowship as though the offense never happened, are we then to resume life as before? Yes, and no. Yes, we are to *treat* the offender as though it never happened just as God does us; and yes, we must actively confirm our love to Him. No, granting forgiveness does not mean it is always possible to restore immediately the trust that was destroyed or the conditions that were present before the offense.

For instance, to restore a repentant pedophile to his nursery school position even after he genuinely repents would be unwise. We are not to have a hateful attitude toward him. We are not to treat him differently than before. But we would be unwise to put him in a position where he would be tempted to repeat his sin.

Forgiveness does not imply that the consequences can be disregarded. Some sins require consequences such as serving time in the judicial system for crimes. However, we are to actively confirm our love to the offender and do everything we can to restore him to a fruitful Christian life as long as there is no evidence of rebellion in his life toward God.

Too often we withhold love and acceptance to a repentant brother or sister, or impose conditions that are not appropriate, merciful, or kind. Our place is not to punish or inflict hardship designed to make the repentant brother more sorrowful for the wrong done or to remind him of his sin. Any attempt on our part to do this constitutes an unwillingness to forgive or humbly restore one who has sinned.

God warns us, "Shouldest not thou also have had compassion on thy fellow servant, even as I had pity on thee? And his lord was wroth, and delivered him to the tormentors…So likewise shall my heavenly Father do also unto you, if ye from your hearts forgive not every one his brother their trespasses" (*Matthew 18:33-35*). When we make a deliberate choice to harbor grudges or withhold forgiveness and reconciliation, we put ourselves in serious spiritual peril. Our mental institutions and hospitals are filled with people who have been "delivered to the tormentors" because they refuse to relinquish anger and bitterness or forgive. Many a suffering saint could be released from his lonely prison of mental anguish if he would simply repent of his pride and choose to forgive as God forgives.

We Alone are Responsible for our Attitude

Making a choice to relinquish all grudges against an offender is not saying the offense was insignificant or that the offender should be released from being held responsible for his actions. We may need to give up resentment against an offender for sins committed against us that were truly wicked and harmful to us, sins God hates, sins God will judge, sins for which He will hold the person responsible.

Even when those who wrong us do not repent, we can be absolutely confident that God is in control of our life. Our loving heavenly Father promises He will use even the very painful sins of others, the very sins He will ultimately judge, to accomplish His good purposes in our life.

When we choose not to hold a grudge, we are merely saying we are willing to trust God and place the judging and execution of justice in His hands alone. We are released from the turmoil of our own bitterness and resentment when we choose to forgive.

Refusing to give up resentments only destroys our own soul, not the person's soul who wronged us. People who have mistreated us are *not* responsible for our unhappiness. Our misery is *not* their problem. Our resentment is *our* problem and *our* sinful response that keeps us unhappy.

As long as we assume other people are responsible for our unhappiness, we refuse to acknowledge our own responsibility to trust God and respond to offenses in the right way. Blaming people who wrong us for our unhappiness keeps us miserable and blind and resentful. But when we learn to relinquish our grudges by committing our case to God, a wonderful change takes place in our own hearts. And sometimes, the change that occurs in our heart and in our attitude begins to alter the attitude and behavior of our offender.

What to Do When You Are Wronged

Step One

Clarify the wrong committed against you in Biblical terms. Exactly what wrong was committed? Is it an offense as Scripture defines sin, or is it an offense arising from carnal expectations and self-centeredness? Are you overreacting to someone's efforts to address a problem that is yours?

Proverbs 3:30—Strive not with a man without cause, if he have done thee no harm.

Romans 12:18—If it be possible, as much as lieth in you, live peaceably with all men.

Romans 14:19—Let us therefore follow after the things which make for peace, and things wherewith one may edify another.

Step Two

Consider your own responsibility about the offense in the light of God's Word. Confess it, and repent of it. Do not go to your offender if you have the motive to hurt him, to retaliate, or to vent anger. Your motive must always be to restore the relationship and the offender, and your attitude must always be one of love and kindness. Remember, it is much easier to be honest about others than it is to be honest about yourself.

Matthew 7:3-5—And why beholdest thou the mote that is in thy brother's eye, but considerest not the beam that is in thine own eye? Or how wilt thou say to thy brother, Let me pull out the mote out of thine eye; and, behold, a beam is in thine own eye? Thou hypocrite, first cast out the beam out of thine own eye; and then shalt thou see clearly to cast out the mote out of they brother's eye.

Galatians 6:1—Brethren, if a man be overtaken in a fault, ye which are spiritual, restore such a one in the spirit of meekness; considering thyself, lest thou also be tempted.

Step Three

Lovingly and humbly confront the offender concerning the wrong he committed against you.

Matthew 18:15-16—Moreover if thy brother shall trespass against thee, go and tell him his fault between thee and him alone; if he shall hear thee, thou hast gained thy brother. But if he will not hear thee, the take with thee one or two more, that in the mouth of two or three witnesses every word may be established.

Luke 17:3-4—Take heed to yourselves; if thy brother trespass against thee, rebuke him; and if he repent, forgive him. And if he trespass against thee seven times in a day, and seven times in a day turn again to thee, saying, I repent; thou shalt forgive him.

Ephesians 4:25—Wherefore putting away lying, speak every man truth with his neighbor; for we are members one of another.

Step Four

If your offender acknowledges the wrong and accepts responsibility* for his actions, you are commanded to forgive him immediately.

Forgiving means

- You promise you will not bring up the offense again to accuse, punish, or humiliate him.

- You promise you will not allow yourself to dwell upon the offense.

- You promise you will not hold the offense against the offender.

Ephesians 4:32—Be ye kind one to another, tenderhearted, forgiving one another, even as God for Christ's sake hath forgiven you.

Colossians 3:13—Forbearing one another, and forgiving one another, if any man have a quarrel against any; even as Christ forgave you, so also do ye.

*Accepting responsibility for sinful actions in the case of serious sin, or a crime having been committed, would mean the offender is willing to accept the judicial repercussions of his sin, or submit to pastoral leadership for help in establishing changes leading to a life of credibility and victory.

You Must Forgive

The following is from *Baker Dictionary of Theology*:

"If your offender is willing to repent and acknowledge wrong, you MUST be willing to forgive him and restore fellowship with him. We are to forgive on the basis of how God has loved and forgiven us freely, not on the basis of whether or not it is deserved or whether we feel like it or not. Remember, we did not, and do not, deserve God's forgiveness. He gives it to us freely and immediately the moment we repent and ask for it. We are to do exactly the same. If we do not, serious consequences will follow. Forgiveness is an act of obedience, not something we wait to do when we *feel* like' it. The feelings of love and forgiveness eventually follow the *act* of forgiveness *after* we work to restore the relationship. When we are reconciled with one another, enmity and alienation are replaced by peace and fellowship.

Matthew 6:14-15—If ye forgive men their trespasses, your heavenly Father will also forgive you: but if ye forgive not men their trespasses, neither will your Father forgive your trespasses.

Matthew 18:33-35—Shouldest not thou also have had compassion on thy fellow servant, even as I had pity on thee? And his lord was wroth, and delivered him to the tormentors, till he should pay all that was due unto him. So likewise shall my heavenly father do also unto you, if ye from your hearts forgive not every one his brother their trespasses.

Appeal Refused

In most cases, if your appeal is refused, you will need to leave the matter entirely with the Lord and go on. Remember, love covers a multitude of sins, and it is our glory to pass over a transgression. Your attitude should be one of love, kindness, and trust in God, knowing God has promised to judge righteously in our behalf if we will commit our case to Him in this way.

1 Thessalonians 4:6—That no man go beyond and defraud (oppress) his brother in any matter; because that the Lord is the avenger of all such, as we also have forewarned you and testified. For God hath not called us unto uncleanness, but unto holiness. He therefore that despiseth, despiseth not man, but God, who hath also given unto us his Holy Spirit.

Colossians 3:24-25—Knowing that of the Lord ye shall receive the reward of the inheritance; for ye serve the Lord Christ; but he that doeth wrong shall receive for the wrong which he hath done; and there is no respect of persons.

Romans 12:19—Dearly beloved, avenge not yourselves, but rather give place unto wrath; for it is written, Vengeance is mine; I will repay, saith the Lord.

A Serious Matter

In very serious matters, if the offender repeatedly refuses to acknowledge wrong, bring another godly person with you to confront him. If he still does not acknowledge his sin and repent, take the matter to your pastor and allow him to give you wise counsel. Then deal with the problem as your pastor chooses.

Matthew 18:17—And if he shall neglect to hear them, tell it unto the church; but if he neglect to hear the church, let him be unto thee as an heathen man and a publican.

Luke 6:27-34—But I say unto you which hear, Love your enemies, do good to them which hate you, bless them that curse you, and pray for them which despitefully use you. And unto him that smiteth thee on the *one* cheek offer also the other; and him that taketh away thy cloke forbid not *to take thy* coat also. Give to every man that asketh of thee; and of him that taketh away thy goods ask *them* not again. And as ye would that men should do to you, do ye also to them likewise. For if ye love them which love you, what thank have ye? For sinners also love those that love them. And if ye do good to them which do good to you, what thank have ye? For sinners also do even the same. And if ye lend *to them* of whom ye hope to receive, what thank have ye? For sinners also lend to sinners, to receive as much again.

Proverbs 24:17, 29—Rejoice not when thine enemy falleth, and let not thine heart be glad when he stumbleth. Say not, I will do so to him as he hath done to me; I will render to the man according to his work.

Romans 12:20-21—Therefore if thine enemy hunger, feed him; if he thirst, give him drink; for in so doing thou shalt heap coals of fire on his head. Be not overcome of evil, but overcome evil with good.

For further help in the area of forgiveness, Dr. John Vaughn, pastor of Faith Baptist Church in Greenville, South Carolina, has an excellent sermon series titled *Forgiveness*. You can order his 6 audio-taped messages by contacting Faith Baptist Church, 500 West Lee Road, Taylors, SC 29687, (864) 322-0700.

Lesson 6

The Joy of Christian Womanhood - Part I

Blessed are they that keep His testimonies, and
that seek Him with the whole heart.
Psalm 119:2

Thy testimonies have I taken as heritage forever,
for they are the rejoicing of my heart.
Psalm 119:111

Key Thoughts

JOY
Confidence in God's love and purpose for me

DISILLUSIONMENT AND SORROW
Confusion over God's purpose for me

Research Question: *2 Timothy 3:6 mentions silly women ever learning. What does this phrase mean?*

1. There is a Biblical relationship between being joyful, and being a _____ wife. *Ephesians 5:18-21*

2. When a godly mother diligently teaches her child to love God and to be _____, she enjoys him and is happy. *Proverbs 23:24-25*

3. When a child is willfully disobedient, part of teaching children to be wise involves_____ _____ and _____. *Proverbs 29:15*

4. The woman who seeks _____ with her whole heart is happy. *Psalm 119:2*

5. When a woman _____ she has joy and peace. *Romans 15:13*

6. Happy is the woman who seeks and finds _____. *Proverbs 3:13-18*

*The surest path to happiness is in losing yourself in a cause
greater than yourself.* —Author Unknown

Submitting to Christ

When a woman lovingly submits to the Lordship of Christ and learns to accept the unique responsibilities He has assigned to her, she develops contentment, personal fulfillment, purpose, and happiness as a by-product. Women who try to build their homes and life by any blueprint other than the Lord's ultimately find their plan results in a shaky structure of discontent, frustration, and disharmony.

Making choices contrary to God's plan always ends in sorrow and regret. This misery is never God's intention for His children. God tells us, "I know the thoughts that I think toward you, saith the Lord, thoughts of peace, and not of evil, to give you an expected end" *(Jeremiah 29:11)*. God wants us to discover how trusting Him results in joy and peace. His expected end is always one that is sweet and rewarding. Women are desperately searching for happiness and contentment by improving their standard of living, by improving their relationships, by asserting and grooming every aspect of themselves, or by discovering some new experience. They are, indeed, *"ever learning and never able to come to the knowledge of truth."* Such searching ultimately ends in disappointment. Contentment and happiness cannot be discovered until a woman makes a conscious decision to live to please the Lord rather than living to please herself.

The root of human thirst and discontent springs from a failure to seek and know God. We remain discontent when we become emotionally attached to things, people, achievements, or interests instead of the God who has formed and sustained us. When we do not fall in love with the person of Christ, we do not cultivate an enjoyment for the things of God or the Word of God, which is the well from which we find living water, our source for wisdom and joy. (Study *Psalm 63* and *John 4:7-15*.)

A woman without wisdom fails to recognize the philosophies of the world that are frequently in direct opposition to the desires and commands of God for His people. Consequently, she is often unknowingly seduced and weakened or destroyed by these philosophies. The world would have us to believe that God withholds happiness and delights in a morbid life of suffering and the denial of anything we might desire. Nothing could be further from the truth. Listen to God's lament for people who rejected His ways to follow their own.

"I am the Lord thy God, which brought thee out of the land of Egypt: open thy mouth wide, and I will fill it. But My people would not hearken to My voice; and Israel would none of Me. So I gave them up unto their own hearts' lust; and they walked in their own counsels. Oh that My people had hearkened unto Me, and Israel had walked in My ways! I should soon have subdued their enemies, and turned My hand

against their adversaries...He should have fed them also with the finest of the wheat; and with honey out of the rock should I have satisfied thee" *(Psalm 82:10-16)*.

God's ways, in contrast to man's ways, produce the happiness we truly desire. "Oh taste and see that the Lord is good! Blessed [Blessed means happy!] is the man that trusteth in Him" *(Psalm 34:8)*.

God's Plan for Women vs. The Feminist Philosophy

Paul says in *Titus 2:4-5*, "...that they [older, spiritually mature women] may teach the young women to be sober, to love their husbands, to love their children, to be discreet, chaste, keepers at home, good, obedient to their own husbands, that the Word of God be not blasphemed."

Being Sober—stable, sensible, wise

God wants us to know Him personally. Wisdom comes from understanding the fear of the Lord and applying our hearts to know God's Word. We must recognize that true wisdom comes only from God. The benefits and riches of godly wisdom are innumerable!

The feminist counterfeit minimizes or scorns godly wisdom and instead glorifies the riches of worldly wisdom—a degree, extended education, and social status. Feminism has made pride and arrogance a virtue. (For further study: *Proverbs 14:1; Proverbs 2:1-12; Hebrews 5:14; Ecclesiastes 8:1,5; Isaiah 33:6; Psalm 107:43; Proverbs 3:13, 18; Proverbs 16:16-22; 2 Peter 1:2; James 1:5; Psalm 110:10; Proverbs 14:6; Psalm 25:12; Daniel 12:3 - Proverbs 31:30-31*)

<u>God's Way</u>   <u>Feminist's Way</u>

Know God. Know Yourself.   Educate Yourself.

Loving Your Husband—unconditional devotion and delight; affectionate; fond of man; a friend and companion

The love spoken of in this passage is not the romantic love that often initially attracts us to a particular man and creates in us a desire for marriage or the commitments of marriage. This love is committed, unconditional love intentionally cultivated within the intimacy of marriage. It is the mature love and acceptance of genuine friendship intertwined with the affectionate love of a sweetheart. It involves a deliberate decision and choice to love and to commit acts of love.

To love our husbands means we are deliberately choosing to deny ourselves in order to fulfill the Biblical role of being a unique helper to our husband. God created and equipped women to complement and complete a man, to be a companion with him for life. *Genesis 2:18* says, "And the LORD God said, It is not good that the man should be alone; I will make him an help meet [or suitable] for him." How we help our husbands depends a great deal on his needs, his life work, his unique personality, his particular abilities and disabilities.

The feminist philosophy, on the other hand, encourages women to put themselves first, to assert their independence, to liberate themselves from the concept of a relationship where two become one and operate as a team. When the oneness of a marriage is lost, the sweetness of godly intimacy is lost as well. (For further study: *Genesis 2:18; Matthew 7:12; 1 John; Solomon 7:6; Hebrews 13:4; 1 Corinthians 7:3-5; Proverbs 5:15-19; Proverbs 27:17; 1 Corinthians 13*)

God's Way	Feminist's Way
Deny Yourself	Liberate Yourself

Loving Your Children—maternal affection (tender feelings); sensitive to; devotion for; fond of; loving with patient understanding and purpose

The word *love* as it is used in *Titus 2:4-5* implies more than a mother's natural instinct to nourish and care for her own children. This love is to be cultivated, taught, and developed in much the same way love toward husbands is cultivated. It is more than the act of loving. It is the *art* of choosing to love and shape the life of one's child *selflessly*.

This kind of love and patience is produced by the Holy Spirit in the heart of a mother that is yielded to and dependent on God (*Galatians 5*). A wise mother realizes loving her children will require her to sacrificially invest the time, discipline, and attention that they need. A mother who loves her children in the godly sense will not hesitate to lose herself in the task of daily teaching principles and skills that will prepare her children to live a godly and productive life.

Page 73

She realizes *well-behaved children do not just happen,* and accepts the time-consuming responsibility of teaching them self-control and godly disciplines. She does not regard her children as an inconvenience in her life, nor does she regard her investment in their care as demeaning or unworthy of her sacrifice. She gladly denies pleasing herself in order to provide for the needs of her children.

Feminists abhor such behavior, labeling it co-dependency, a waste, martyrdom, or even pathological. God, however, highly esteems this unconditional love and calls it wise. The godly mother asks, "What is best for the children God has entrusted to my care?" The unbelieving mother asks, "What is, first of all, best for me?" The believing mother declares, "By God's grace and strength I can." The unbelieving mother declares, "I can't." (For further study: *Proverbs 23:24-25; 1 Peter 3:8; Proverbs 19:18; Proverbs 29:15; Isaiah 28:9-10; Colossians 3:21; Deuteronomy 6:6-7; Psalm 78:4-8*)

God's Way	Feminist's Way
Lose Yourself	Find Yourself

***Being Discreet**—self-controlled; self-disciplined; curbing desires, impulses, and opinions*

The most common cause or starting point of depression is a subtle sense of guilt, self-pity, and/or anger that is being fed by some kind of irresponsible behavior or self-indulgence. Responsible, disciplined behavior produces a sense of well being and contentment.

However, irresponsible, indulgent behavior produces a sense of despair and defeat. God knew what He was doing when He instructed the older women to teach the younger to learn self-control and self-discipline!

The feminist philosophy of indulging every craving of the flesh and gratifying every whim does not produce happiness. Contrary—the psychologist's offices are exploding with cases of women suffering from depression and anxiety-related disorders because of underlying refusals to control one's thoughts, desires, and impulses. (For further study: *Proverbs 4:23; Romans 13:14; 2 Corinthians 10:5; Galatians 5:16; Colossians 3:1-17*)

God's Way	Feminist's Way
Control Yourself	Indulge Yourself

Lesson 7

The Joy of Christian Womanhood - Part II

Strength and honor are her clothing; and she shall
rejoice in time to come.
Proverbs 31:25

Give her of the fruit of her hands; and let her own
works praise her in the gates.
Proverbs 31:31

Key Thoughts

A Sense of Well Being and Joy
Guiding my home and personal life responsibly and in a godly way

Discontentment and Irritability
Neglecting the needs of my family and failing to develop spiritual accomplishments in my life

---

Research Question: *1 Timothy* uses the phrase "to guide the home." What does this mean?

1. If a woman chooses to invest labor and time building her home and family God's way, she will reap the benefits of her labor and it will _____ _____ _____ _____. *Psalm 128:2*

2. God is able to make a woman a _____ mother of children. *Psalm 113:9*

3. A godly Christian mother has no greater joy than when she sees her children _____ ___ ____ _____. *3 John 1:4*

4. Women who exercise godly _____ are joyful. *Proverbs 21:15*

5. It is a _____ for a woman to give herself to the cause of Christ and even sacrifice for the sake of others. *Philippians 2:17*

Loving others makes us happy. Loving ourselves makes us lonely. —Author Unknown

Being Chaste—clean; innocent; modest; morally pure; consecrated

To be chaste implies something we *are*, not some way in which we are to *act*. It is a total change of lifestyle that is the direct result of a change deep within the heart. In particular, being chaste is the outcome of a daily relationship with the Lord Jesus Christ.

Adopting high standards of living to please or appease another person or in an effort to make ourselves feel more spiritual is dangerous. Christians who do this do not fully understand that righteousness cannot be earned but is wholly received by faith in Christ. Paul confirms this truth in *Philippians 3:9*. "And be found in Him, not having mine own righteousness, which is of the law, but that which is through the faith of Christ, the righteousness which is of God by faith." Taking pride, or glorying, in acts of holiness leads to an obnoxious and self-righteous attitude. Paul warns, "But he that glorieth, let him glory in the Lord. For not he that commendeth himself is approved, but whom the Lord commendeth" (*2 Corinthians 10:17-18*).

We do not *clean up our act* and do righteous acts for others to see as though righteous acts are the things which make us spiritual. Rather, we are to clean up our heart and grow in our knowledge of the Lord so we will become spiritually minded. Our righteous acts and obedience are then a spontaneous outflow of that changed and obedient heart that is in fellowship with Christ. Paul recognized that in himself, he was nothing. Only as a result of faith in Christ and God's work in his life could he say, "by the grace of God I am what I am" (*1 Corinthians 15:10*). The knowledge that Christ (and not ourselves) makes us holy leads to an attitude of humility and thankfulness.

The woman who grows in grace and develops inner beauty will reflect spiritual qualities in all her outward actions. It is the woman who lives in harmony and dependence on the Holy Spirit who does not fulfill the selfish desires of her human nature (*Galatians 5:16*). To such a woman, godliness is a delight and fulfills her natural desire to be both feminine and pure by God's design. Virtues such as modesty or moral purity are something she is, not something she wears or does. Because she *is* modest and *is* pure in heart, she clothes herself modestly and guards herself from impure thoughts and actions. The woman who chooses to be godly for all the right reasons will find contentment in her lifestyle and discover a host of benefits that will follow her throughout eternity. "Godliness with contentment is great gain" (*1 Timothy 6:6*).

The feminist philosophy, in contrast, mocks a modest, consecrated woman. It openly promotes abandoning restraint and indulging in sensuality and immoral thoughts and actions. God says to be chaste; the world says to be sensuous. (For further study: *Matthew 5:8; 2 Corinthians 10:5; Proverbs 31:26; 1 Timothy 2:9-10; Proverbs 13:20*)

NOTES

God's Way	Feminist's Way
Draw attention to God	Draw attention to Yourself

Being a Keeper at Home—working at home; domestic guardian of the home; guiding, caring for, managing the home

Where a woman chooses to focus her primary attention and give the greatest portion of her life usually indicates where she intends to find her greatest fulfillment and happiness. The way we invest our time and money reveals a great deal about the condition and priorities of our hearts (*Matthew 6:21*). It is not difficult to spot women who passionately believe the guidance and management of the home is so important that it determines the future moral, economical, and spiritual success of families, churches, and countries. Such women spend a great deal of time and effort working on their home life and strengthening the homes of others.

Throughout Scripture, women are recognized as being multi-talented, capable, co-laborers of God who were often responsible for influencing the hearts of kings and nations and for establishing the strength of character and moral fiber of whole generations of people. These Bible women did not accidentally or casually influence their families for good; they deliberately gave their lives for that noble purpose. Whatever else they were or whatever else these women accomplished, they were first and foremost the guardians of their home.

When a woman begins to believe that her unique role as *keeper at home* is less important than an occupation or that it is a task unworthy of her diligence, skill, and intelligence, she trades the most eternally rewarding endeavor of womankind for a temporal and inferior occupation. She may likely be embarrassed to be called wife, mother, or homemaker; and she may find it much more rewarding to be known by a professional title or achievement. While the world applauds such a woman, Heaven pities her; for they who see what we can only know by faith know the future loss of those who fail to put God's priorities first. Moses made a deliberate choice to reject the titles, privileges, and esteem of Egyptian nobility. He chose instead to identify with the despised and "worthless" Hebrew slaves. Moses decided that the temporary honor of being identified as the son of Pharaoh was not worth forfeiting the honor and riches awaiting those in Heaven who were not ashamed to be identified with Christ (*Hebrews 11:24-26*). The woman who cannot comprehend the eternal value of building a truly committed Christian home cannot comprehend the ultimate joy of sacrificing for its welfare.

Feminists disdain the notion that an intelligent woman could be fulfilled in centering her life on her home. Instead, they encourage women to be *me* centered, and reduce *home* to a place where the family sleeps, eats, and displays their earthly belongings. (For further study: *Proverbs 31*)

God's Way	Feminist's Way
Humble Yourself	Elevate Yourself

Doing Good—virtuous; benevolent; producing good works

The feminist philosophy promotes an attitude that assumes the chief end of woman is to have fun and enjoy life. Self-fulfillment is exalted as a cause worth living for. God in His wisdom tells us otherwise. The chief end of all people is to glorify God by loving Him and loving others. It is a deception to believe *having fun* produces inner joy or contentment. Having fun does not produce lasting joy and contentment. Fun certainly has its place and purpose. To be able to laugh and enjoy living are gifts from God, but having fun is not the purpose of life. Nor should fun become the driving goal in a Christian's life. The woman who wants genuine joy seeks to be benevolent and produce good works. She *knows* "…we are his workmanship, created in Christ Jesus unto good works, which God hath before ordained that we should walk in them" (*Ephesians 2:10*). And, "… these things I will that thou affirm constantly, that they which have believed in God might be careful to maintain good works. These things are good and profitable unto men" (*Titus 3:8*).

Good works include:

- soul winning (*Proverbs 11:30*)

- nurturing children (*1 Timothy 5:10*)

- supporting husband's life work (*Proverbs 31:11, 31*)

- supporting the weak (*Romans 15:1-2*)

- teaching and discipling (*Titus 2:3*)

- keeping a good testimony (*Titus 2:7*)

- providing basic needs for others when necessary (*James 2:15-17*)

- encouraging brothers and sisters in Christ (*Hebrews 6:10*)

- relieving the hurting or afflicted (*1 Timothy 5:10*)

- exercising faith toward God (*1 Thessalonians 1:3*)

- using talents and spiritual gifts to build your local church (*Ephesians 4:7*)

God's Way	Feminist's Way
Give Yourself	Enjoy Yourself

Obeying Your Husband—subordinate to; under authority of; maintaining respect and reverence for

Perhaps no other aspect of Christian womanhood is more misunderstood or distorted than the command *obey your husband*! The unsaved woman tends to react to such a statement with outrage or disgust and often cannot get past the word *obey* to see the complete picture. Christian women sometimes struggle with the idea of willfully subordinating themselves to a husband as well.

The tendency is either to ignore the word altogether, change its meaning so it is more palatable, or make the word *obey* say something it does not. Can we possibly imagine God really meant *obey* when He said, "obey"? The fact is God said exactly what He wanted to say when He commanded us to be in obedience to our husbands! While submission to our husband's authority might be a difficult concept to swallow at first glance, submission makes perfect sense if we examine it in light of other equally important Scriptural principles.

When we see obedience in its context of faith and the family structure, submission becomes not only the ultimate paradox, but also a great privilege for Christian women. We are able to gladly obey God's command as Sarah did, when we believe God Himself is good and His commandments are for our benefit (*1 Peter 3:6*). Christian women are able to accept the concept of submission without undue amazement because we know that freedom and liberation are ultimately discovered through the act of submission to God.

Submission to a husband is primarily an expression of love and submission to God. God did not command husbands to *make* their wives obey them. Obedience is to be a voluntary act on the part of a believing wife. When she first gives herself to God, she is then able to joyfully give herself to serve others as God commands. Paul applies this principle when he describes the sacrifices and obedience of the Macedonian Christians on his behalf. He said, "And this they did, not as we hoped, but first gave their own selves to the Lord, and unto us by the will of God" (*2 Corinthians 8:5*). When we read this passage in its full context, we can see that the Macedonians ministered to Paul and others as an expression of their great love and thankfulness to God. Love conquers fear (*1 John 4:18*) and propels us to delight in sacrificing for the object of our affection.

Obedient does not mean passive, it means submissive to a husband's right to final authority in an attitude of respect and humility. The Greek word translated *obey* is actually a military term which means, "to be ranked under in military order." That means, the wife may be the sergeant, but her husband has been appointed general! We are to respect this God-given position of leadership

To obey does not mean women are worth less or are in any way inferior to men. It *does* mean women are to assume a different role than men. It *does* mean women are to willingly give up their inclination to control or rule over men as the man's authority. To reverence our husband means we give him respect in an attitude of quietness, not because he always deserves it, but because God commands respect and we delight to demonstrate faith and love toward our Savior. Biblical submission to our husbands is an attitude we choose because God meant it for our good. It is not to be a duty we perform with resentful resignation.

God gives husbands a measure of authority for the harmony of the home and care of the family. As God commands citizens to submit to judicial authority, and Christians to submit to church authority, he commands wives to submit to their husband's authority—in everything. He tells all believers to "obey them that have the rule over you, and submit yourselves: for they watch for your souls, as they that must give account, that they may do it with joy, and not with grief: for that is unprofitable for you" (*Hebrews 13:17*). Even so, the serious Bible student understands that no pastor, deacon, or church leader has been given *absolute* authority, which requires unquestioned submission of church members. A husband's authority, like any other authority God commands that we be in submission to, is *never* an authority that supersedes His own authority. Absolute, sovereign authority belongs to God and God alone (*Matthew 28:18*).

A husband has no God-given right to command his wife to violate any command of God, nor does he possess authority that gives him a right to demand his wife submit passively to evil, or to destruction that he perpetrates. Obeying God's command to preserve life and to protect the helpless must take precedence over a wonderfully true principle that applies *except* when wives, and sometimes even the children, are in real danger—spiritually, emotionally, and physically (*Micah 6:8; Acts 20:35; Romans 15:1; 1 Thessalonians 5:14*). Those under submission to another are never to submit passively to sin, but neither are they to arrogantly defy an authority in anger or contempt. Those under authority are to make a godly appeal after the pattern of Daniel, Esther, Paul, and Peter and only then humbly choose to obey God rather than man (*Acts 5:29; 4:19–20*).

A believing wife's proper attitude of humility and submission toward an unbelieving

NOTES

and difficult husband has the capability of softening his heart toward the Gospel (*1 Peter 3:1-6*). The self-willed and rebellious Christian wife tends to provoke resentment in her husband toward the Lord. Rather than demonstrating the power and love of God in her life, she displays hypocrisy and arrogance. Even the lost are repelled by pride and softened by humility. Sometimes the godly behavior of a loving wife breaks the hold of sin on an unbelieving husband. The believing wife needs to pattern her love after God's. God tells us, "Or despiseth thou the riches of his goodness and forbearance and longsuffering; not knowing that the goodness of God leadeth thee to repentance?" (*Romans 2:4*).

Winning a husband by demonstrating a humble spirit and godly behavior does not mean that if a woman is submissive and loving enough, the husband will always change, without any other action or intervention. Nor does it mean that God has promised to transform the marriage if the wife has the right motives, faith, and so on. Sometimes husbands do not have a change of heart toward God or their wife unless serious, active intervention takes place. In many cases, the husband never repents and never experiences change, no matter how godly, loving, and submissive the wife is. A wife cannot know whether or not an unbelieving husband will be saved (*1 Corinthians 7:16*). Therefore, she is to do all in her power to influence him by her loving and righteous behavior, knowing God rewards her faith and love whether or not her husband repents.

Obedience is pleasing to God regardless of how our husbands respond. Because submission is pleasing to God and requires faith, it is a great accomplishment of God's power and grace in our lives. Submission for the right reasons produces an inner joy and contentment that, quite frankly, doesn't make sense to the feminist crowd. Women who choose to submit themselves develop a meek (humble, controlled strength) and quiet (content, peaceful) spirit. Women who choose to assert themselves in defiance tend to develop an angry, resentful spirit. (For further study: *Colossians 3:18; Luke 6:46; 1 Corinthians 11:3; 1 Corinthians 11:7-9; 1 Timothy 2:12-14; Ephesians 5:22-24, 33; 1 Peter 2; 1 Peter 3; Matthew 6:24; 1 John 3:22; Psalm 111:10; Matthew 5:19; 1 John 5:3*)

God's Way	Feminist's Way
Submit Yourself	Exalt Yourself

Joyful Christian Womanhood Inventory Sheet

No woman has "arrived" and no woman has fully mastered all the disciplines of a truly godly life. It is our joy to find comfort in knowing we are God's little children who are day by day growing in grace, wholly dependent on our Father's love and care. He does not overwhelm us with unreasonable demands or require maturity beyond our capability. *Micah 6:8* says, "He hath showed thee, O man, what is good; and what doth the Lord require of thee, but to do justly, and to love mercy, and to walk humbly with thy God." Following is a list that is not intended to discourage you; it is intended to provoke you to love and to good works as you daily walk with God and look to Him for help and direction in your personal life. Failures in areas such as these often lead to unhappiness and a sense of personal failure. Mark those that are a problem for you and then seek God's help and direction as you work to grow in these areas.

NOTES

Wisdom

_____ I am keeping a regular devotion time with the Lord (Bible reading and prayer).

_____ I do not doubt God's love for me.

_____ I do not doubt God is in control of my life.

_____ I do not doubt my salvation.

_____ My prayers do not revolve predominately around myself.

_____ I know I am not doing something that displeases God.

_____ I have a desire for God's wisdom and am diligently seeking it.

Love for my Husband

(Include your husband when you answer the questions concerning him.)

_____ I encourage and help my husband in several specific ways.

_____ My husband is pleased with the efforts I make to be physically attractive to him.

_____ I am cultivating a mutually satisfying physical relationship with my husband.

_____ My husband is happy with the companionship I provide for him.

_____ My husband is satisfied with the domestic support I provide for him.

Love for my Children

_____ I am actively involved in teaching my children to love the Lord and enjoy His ways.

_____ I spend time talking to each of my children individually every day.

_____ I am interested and involved in helping my children pursue their special interests and talents.

_____ I teach my children specific skills on a regular basis.

_____ I consistently and confidently insist my children respect and obey me.

_____ I do not hesitate to use corporal punishment (properly applied) for deliberate defiance (disobedience).

_____ I do not lose my temper or use corporal punishment for childish infractions that do not involve willful disobedience.

_____ I am actively involved in encouraging and helping my children learn how to succeed and achieve goals.

Discretion

_____ My house is cleaned each day.

_____ I control what I eat.

_____ I exercise regularly.

_____ I am content with my daily activities and accomplishments.

_____ I accomplish specific goals each week.

_____ I get up at a specific time.

_____ I do not often regret things I say.

Chaste

_____ I refrain from watching soap operas.

_____ I refrain from watching more than four hours of TV each week.

_____ I refrain from wearing clothing in public that makes me feel sexually appealing.

_____ I refrain from daydreaming or fantasizing about things I would be embarrassed to tell anyone about.

_____ I refrain from reading literature or books I would not want the preacher to see.

_____ I do not talk about things or tell jokes I would be embarrassed for someone to hear.

_____ I enjoy living a godly life and identifying with women who love God and avoid worldliness.

Home

_____ I work hard to make my home a pleasant, happy place for my family.

_____ I enjoy learning and cultivating a variety of homemaking skills.

_____ I enjoy working at home.

_____ I use my home for hospitality and projects that benefit others.

_____ I regularly prepare meals at home and make mealtime enjoyable for my family.

Good

_____ I recognize that spending time loving and training my children is an important ministry that pleases God.

_____ I enjoy helping and encouraging others.

_____ I regularly take advantage of opportunities to witness and win others to the Lord.

_____ I pray for other church members regularly.

_____ I share a portion of my time and material blessings with others.

_____ I know my spiritual gift(s) and am developing them.

_____ I am involved in some kind of ministry through my church.

Obedient

_____ I express appreciation to my husband regularly.

_____ I do not discuss my husband's flaws or faults with others.

_____ I cheerfully obey my husband without fighting with him.

_____ I know how to appeal or disagree with my husband in a calm and respectful manner.

_____ I seek my husband's prayer, opinions, and direction.

_____ I allow my husband to make mistakes without humiliating him or putting him down.

NOTES

Lesson 8

THE JOY OF OVERCOMING DISAPPOINTMENTS

Casting all your care upon Him: for He careth for you.
1 Peter 5:7

My soul, wait thou only upon God; for my expectation is from Him. He only is my rock and my salvation; He is my defense; I shall not be moved.
Psalm 62:5-6

Key Thoughts

A Thankful and Joyful Heart
Results as I guide my home and personal life responsibly and in a godly way

A Bitter Heart
Results as I neglect the needs of my family and fail to develop spiritual accomplishments in my life

---

Research Question: *1 Peter 5:7* and *Psalm 55:22* mention that we are to cast our care on God. What does this mean?

1. From time to time a woman's _____ can actually be a good thing for her. *Ecclesiastes 7:3-4*

2. A woman can even be happy when the Lord corrects her because she knows _____. *Hebrews 12:9-11*

3. When a woman thinks on _____, she becomes satisfied and happy. *Psalm 63:5-7*

4. A woman can rejoice even when she is treated unfairly because _____. *Luke 6:22-23*

5. A godly woman can have joy even in times of adversity if she _____. *1 Peter 1:8*

When you have nothing left but God, then for the first time you become aware that God is enough. — Maude Royden

Our View of Disappointments

Try as we might, none of us escape disappointments. We experience disappointment when rain spoils a family picnic, when a friend betrays our confidence, when our tax return isn't as large as we had hoped, or when a favorite sweater is ruined in the dryer. Most of us learn to expect disappointments like these, knowing they are a normal part of life in an imperfect world among imperfect people. While events such as these certainly.make it a "bad hair day," they aren't usually enough to derail us emotionally or cause significant sorrow. In fact, if disappointments were never any worse than a rained out picnic, we could laugh them all off as the cost of being human. Not all disappointments provide good material for humor, however. Some are difficult to overcome. Others are excruciatingly painful and change a life forever.

Life's disappointments come in all colors and varieties, some darker than others. A failed marriage, a broken engagement, the premature death of a loved one, a ruined career, or a wayward child all crush hopes and dreams that have been cherished or long anticipated. Some make us feel as though the rug has been yanked out from under us—others leave us dumbfounded or numb with pain. Yet these kinds of disappointments are as much a part of life as a rainy day or a bad haircut. None of us are exempt from them. Since this is a common part of life, shall we resign ourselves to a painful existence and expect our life to be one long emotional roller coaster ride? Absolutely not. While disappointments of every kind are inevitable, its ill effects are not.

A Biblical perspective greatly diminishes the pain of disappointments and turns many into blessings in disguise, or opportunities for growth and change. How we view our disappointments makes all the difference in the world in how they will affect us. When we experience a disappointment, to some degree we are experiencing the death of hopes and desires of some kind. The very nature of disappointment depends on the place of importance we give an expectation or the level of desire that precedes it. If we did not care or did not have a particular expectation, we would not be disappointed. When our greatest dreams and desires depend on uncertain circumstances or imperfect people, we are undoubtedly headed for suffering and despair.

There is no person, no achievement, and no hope of earthly pleasure that is certain to fulfill our dreams or live up to our greatest expectations. Nothing in this life can be depended upon or provide the security and enjoyment that our hearts long for. God did not design us with the capacity to be fulfilled by things that are found on this earth. David understood this when He cried out to God, "Whom have I in Heaven but thee? And there is none upon earth that I desire beside thee. My flesh and my heart faileth: but God is the strength of my heart, and my portion for ever" (*Psalm 73:25-26*).

God is the only Person in the world who will never disappoint us, never change, never leave us, never break a promise, and never let us down. His love will never fail us; He will never say an unkind thing to us; and He will never misjudge or misunderstand us. He will never lose His patience with us or become weary forgiving us. The treasures He prepares for us in Heaven are not in jeopardy of being lost or stolen. Our hopes and dreams for eternity cannot come close to the reality of its beauty and joy, let alone be taken from us for any reason. When we set our hearts on the things of God, we set our hearts on the one thing that can never disappoint us. No wonder Paul urged us to "set [our] affection on things above, not on things on the earth" (*Colossians 3:2*).

When living for the Lord Jesus Christ is the most important thing in the world to us, life's greatest disappointments become small in comparison to Heaven's rewards. Delighting in God's devotion and shepherding care takes the sting out of life and puts our broken dreams into eternal perspective. What seems like a major calamity on earth is but a fleeting sorrow in light of God's tender love and the eternal significance He gives to our troubles. We can think long upon the sweet and comforting words found in *2 Corinthians 4:16-18*. "For which cause we faint not; but though our outward man perish, yet the inward man is renewed day by day, for our light affliction, which is but for a moment, worketh for us a far more exceeding and eternal weight of glory; while we look not at the things which are seen, but at the things which are not seen; for the things which are seen are temporal; but the things which are not seen are eternal."

One of the churches' most beloved hymns encourages our hearts and reveals the secret of being able to live joyfully even in times of disappointment. The song says, "O soul, are you weary and troubled? No light in the darkness you see? There's light for a look at the Savior, and life more abundant and free! Turn your eyes upon Jesus, look full in His wonderful face, and the things of earth will grow strangely dim in the light of His glory and grace."

Checklist of Disappointments Common to Women

____ I'm not very pretty.

____ I'm not very smart.

____ I'm not as successful as I want to be.

____ I'm not self-disciplined.

____ I'm not financially secure.

____ My children rebel against me.

____ My children are rebelling against the Lord.

____ My children aren't ambitious.

____ My children aren't smart.

NOTES

____ My children aren't very successful.

____ My children aren't popular.

____ I want more children.

____ Being a mother isn't what I thought it would be.

____ My husband isn't as loving as I want him to be.

____ My husband isn't self-controlled.

____ My husband doesn't have the career he wants.

____ My husband isn't very successful.

____ My husband isn't considerate of my feelings.

____ My husband isn't very spiritual.

____ My husband isn't very good with our children.

____ I want a husband.

____ My husband left me.

____ My husband committed adultery.

____ My home isn't very pretty.

____ My home isn't very big.

____ I feel I've failed in many areas.

____ My family or friend has rejected me.

____ I was molested as a child.

____ I've had many financial hardships and/or failures.

____ My health is poor.

____ The health of a family member is poor.

____ My mother or father is hateful toward me.

____ My children don't have a father.

After checking the statements that apply to you, mark and divide them into two categories:

1. Things I cannot change that God wants me to accept.
2. Things God wants me to work to change through His strength, in a Biblical way.

Page 91

Overcoming Disappointment

Note to those using this workbook for a group Bible study: The following list and accompanying Scriptures provide topics for discussion as well as an overview that students will want to review. Students should be challenged to consider which of the following areas give them difficulty and what changes need to take place in their thoughts and beliefs.

Expectations

We automatically trigger feelings of unhappiness when people and situations around us do not *fit our expectations*. Expectations in the wrong things, or inappropriate expectations in the right things, result in unhappiness. Sometimes we look to people to fulfill our needs. We are disappointed when they fail to meet our expectations. God wants us to look to Him, instead. He promises to fulfill every true need we have. Remember that God usually uses people, common circumstances, and everyday events to meet our needs rather than the miraculous or unusual means of intervention that we sometimes look for. When God does not prompt people or circumstances to work out the way we would like or the way we expected, we need to seek the reason from God. God is able to make all grace abound toward us so that every need we have is sufficiently met (*2 Corinthians 9:8*).

Psalm 62:5-6—My soul, wait thou <u>only</u> upon God; for my expectation is from Him. He only is my rock and my salvation; He is my defense; I shall not be moved.

Do I look to God or people to meet my needs? Do I recognize the foolishness of making people my strength instead of God? How do I react when people fail me?

Study *Jeremiah 17:5-8*

Demands

Emotion-backed demands make us suffer, not the world, the people in that world, or the situations in which we find ourselves. External circumstances do not cause us to be unhappy—Our internal demands make us unhappy. (Study *James 4:1-2*.) When our heart's affection is set on what we want rather than what God wants in our lives, we have a tendency to behave in a similar way as the toddler who is denied something he wants in a store. The child's focus is on what he wants. Nothing else matters at that moment for nothing else is as important to him as having the object of his desire.

Hebrew 13:5-6—Let your conversation (behavior) be without covetousness; and be content with such things as ye have; for he hath said, I will never leave thee, nor forsake thee. So that we may boldly say, The Lord is my helper, and I will not fear what man shall do unto me.

Philippians 4:11-13—Not that I speak in respect of want; for I have learned, in whatsoever state I am, therewith to be content. I know both how to be abased, and I know how to abound; everywhere and in all things I am instructed both to be full and to be hungry, both to abound and to suffer need. I can do all things through Christ, which strengtheneth me.

Am I able to give up my desires when they are withheld from me, or do I behave more like the toddler having a temper tantrum when his deepest desires are denied? Am I choosing to set my greatest affection on things that are of eternal significance, or am I concentrating on acquiring things that won't really matter in eternity?

Study *Colossians 3:2*

Sinful Desires

When our expectations become *demands*, we could call them sinful desires. The world, however, would call it an addiction. An addiction, according to secular thinking, is something conditioned into our bodies or our minds that, if not satisfied, automatically triggers a powerful negative emotion. When we develop sinful demands and expectations that are not fulfilled, they do trigger emotions such as anger, fear, jealousy, anxiety, resentment, sorrow, helplessness, or hopelessness. The Bible refers to this as bondage to sin.

Demands are not the same as preferences. Preferences are things we might like to have or have happen, but we don't make them a condition of our happiness. In other words, we won't be unhappy if we don't get what we would like and we certainly won't react with anger or vindictiveness. Demands, however, are things or situations that we believe we *must* have in order to be happy.

1 Peter 4:12-19—Beloved, think it not strange concerning the fiery trial which is to try you, as though some strange thing happened unto you: but rejoice, inasmuch as ye are partakers of Christ's sufferings; that, when His glory shall be revealed, ye may be glad also with exceeding joy. Wherefore, let them that suffer according to the will of God commit the keeping of their souls to Him in well doing, as unto a faithful Creator.

1 Peter 5:6—Humble yourselves therefore under the mighty hand of God, that He may exalt you in due time: casting all your care upon Him; for He careth for you.

Do I have dreams and expectations that I cannot seem to stop thinking about or trying to achieve? Do I become angry or irritable when my desires are withheld or thwarted? Do I brood or become depressed when I am kept from things that are important to me? Have my desires become the main focus of my life?

List Bible characters who became angry or despondent when things didn't turn out the way that they had planned. What can be learned from their actions and reactions?

Priorities

How we react when our desires are withheld or our plans are interrupted often reveals the place of importance we gave to them. If pleasing God and submitting to His will is most important to us, then the loss of all our other desires and plans will not devastate us. But when our own desires and plans are the most important thing to us, we react to their loss with excessive sorrow. Often we refuse to be comforted or to accept the loss. When this occurs, we have sinfully made our expected desires and plans an idol in our life.

An idol is a person or thing that is excessively adored. Idolatry is the giving to any creature or human creation the honor or devotion that belongs to God alone. Idolatry is giving any desire a precedence over God's will. Anything we love more than obeying God has the potential to destroy us. Over and over throughout Israel's history, God told the people to put away their idols "and incline your heart unto the LORD God of Israel" (*Joshua 24:23*). The cure for idolatry is to turn our hearts away from our idolatrous loves (repentance) and turn it to the Lord in loving submission instead.

Ezekiel 14:3-4—Son of man, these men have set up their idols in their heart, and put the stumbling block of their iniquity before their face; should I be inquired of at all by them? Therefore speak unto them, and say unto them, Thus saith the Lord God, Every man of the house of Israel that setteth up his idols in his heart, and putteth the stumbling block of his iniquity before his face, and cometh to the prophet, I the Lord will answer him that cometh according to the multitude of his idols.

Colossians 3:5—Mortify therefore your members which are upon the earth; fornication, uncleanness, inordinate affection, evil concupiscence, and covetousness, which is idolatry.

1 Thessalonians 1:9a—For they themselves show of us what manner of entering in we had unto you, and how ye turned to God from idols to serve the living and true God.

1 John 5:21—Little children, keep yourselves from idols.

What idols of the heart entice me most? What idols would God tell me to keep myself far from?

Study the many incidents in Israel's history where idolatry brought sorrow and withheld God's blessings from God's people.

What are my idols (things I excessively adore; put in precedence over God's will)?

<u>Vanity/Self</u> - Wanting own way; inordinate desire for a position, title, status, security in something besides the Lord (such as friends, credit cards, money, children's success, career success); manifest in sensual clothing or body movements.

<u>Things</u> - House, furnishings, clothes, collectibles

<u>Family</u> - Mom, husband, children

<u>Friends</u> - Improper relationships, attachments; exclusive friends to the exclusion of husband, a relationship with the Lord, or serving and loving the needy and unlovable.

<u>Comfort</u> - Love of pleasure, "escape" in place of love for the work of God; self-indulgence

<u>Helps</u> - Reliance on people, things, circumstances rather than on God; confidence in experts opinions, self-help books in place of confidence in the Bible; reliance on people, or self, in place of trust and reliance on prayer or the Lord; ;ove for socializing, spending time with friends, in place of loving to spend time with the Lord; thankfulness to people for help in place of thankfulness to God.

Trusting God

God promises to meet our needs. There is no reason for us to worry or doubt that God will meet every need connected with our immediate survival. We must simply put God first in our lives and then ask and trust Him for it (*Matthew 6:33*). Everything we enjoy beyond our basic survival needs is a blessing bestowed on us from our God Who delights to bless us abundantly. David assures us that "no good thing will He

withhold from those who walk uprightly" (*Psalm 84:11*). However, when we believe we *have* to have something beyond our basic needs, we've become enslaved (sinfully addicted) to demanding. In reality, our needs are very few.

1 Timothy 6:6-8—But godliness with contentment is great gain. For we brought nothing into this world, and it is certain we can carry nothing out. And having food and raiment let us be therewith content.

Matthew 6:25-33—Therefore I say unto you, Take no thought for your life, what ye shall eat, or what ye shall drink; nor yet for your body, what ye shall put on. Is not the life more than meat, and the body than raiment? Behold the fowls of the air: for they sow not, neither do they reap, nor gather into barns; yet your heavenly Father feedeth them. Are ye not much better than they? Which of you by taking thought can add one cubit unto his stature? And why take ye thought for raiment? Consider the lilies of the field, how they grow; they toil not, neither do they spin: and yet I say unto you, That even Solomon in all his glory was not arrayed like one of these. Wherefore, if God so clothe the grass of the field, which to day is, and to morrow is cast into the oven, shall He not much more clothe you, O ye of little faith? Therefore take no thought, saying, What shall we eat? or, What shall we drink? or, Wherewithal shall we be clothed? For after all these things do the Gentiles seek: for your heavenly Father knoweth that ye have need of all these things. But seek ye first the kingdom of God, and his righteousness; and all these things shall be added unto you.

Do I tend to say "I need" when in reality I should say, "I want" or "I desire"? Do I believe God will give beyond what I need out of love and grace toward me? Am I afraid to ask God for things I desire or afraid to trust God to give or withhold what He knows is best?

Find and identify legitimate "delights" and "idolatrous loves" in the Scriptures. Examples to get you started: *1 Timothy 6:10; John 12:43; Psalm 1:2; Proverbs 29:17*

Manipulation

We keep ourselves unhappy by trying to fulfill our demands in life by getting people and situations to fit our inner programs of security, happiness, pride, or success. Often we end up spending our entire lives trying to manipulate the outside world, and God, in order to be happy. Has it worked? The reason it doesn't work is because acceptance must always precede contentment and happiness. Dependence (resting) on God always precedes spiritual blessings. Learning to accept all that comes into our lives, and depend on God to work things out and meet every one of our needs leads to peace and happiness.

Psalm 37:4—Delight thyself also in the Lord and He shall give thee the desires of thine heart.

James 4:1-3 and 8a—From whence come wars and fightings among you? Come they not hence, even of your lusts that war in your members? Ye lust, and have not; ye kill, and desire to have, and cannot obtain; ye fight and war, yet ye have not, because ye ask not. Ye ask, and receive not, because ye ask amiss, that ye may consume it upon your lusts. Draw nigh to God and he will draw nigh to you.

Romans 8:28—And we know that all things work together for good to them that love God, to them who are the called according to his purpose.

How do I attempt to get people or circumstances to fit my expectations? What is my reaction when they don't "cooperate" with my plans?

Study Sarah's efforts to make things happen her way and its end results.

Making Changes

Instead of wearing ourselves out trying to change the people and situations in our life, we need to concentrate on changing our demands and expectations, the things we believe are our absolute necessities. As we conform our desires to God's desires we will discover that God gives us the desires of our heart.

When we set our affection on the things God desires for us, the sting of disappointments is greatly diminished. While we cannot avoid disappointments that are an inevitable part of life, we *can* learn how to handle them in a way that will bring peace instead of misery.

Psalm 19:12—Who can understand his errors? Cleanse thou me from secret faults.

Psalm 139:23-24—Search me, O God, and know my heart; try me, and know my thoughts; and see if there be any wicked way in me, and lead me in the way everlasting.

Lamentations 3:40—Let us search and try our ways, and turn again to the Lord.

What things do I believe *must* change in order for me to be happy? Can I accept the fact that some problems do not have an answer and will not change? Do I believe that while I cannot change every circumstance or person in my life, I can change me and I can change the way I depend on God to use it in my life for good? Am I willing to let God search my heart and reveal to me the demands and expectations He wants me to change?

Study *Psalm 119* listing the requests David makes to God and the changes He wants God to make in his heart.

Thought Patterns

Our sinful hearts are responsible for our patterns of thinking and behaving. We developed many of our expectations and demands when we were very young. Our mind was very immature, and to a great extent, we were at the mercy of whatever influenced us. However, we are not bound by our "programming"! We are adults who have a God-given capacity and responsibility to change any sinful pattern that has disrupted our Christian joy.

2 Corinthians 5:17—Therefore if any man be in Christ, he is a new creature; old things are passed away; behold, all things are become new.

2 Corinthians 10:4-5—For the weapons of our warfare are not carnal, but mighty through God, to the pulling down of strong holds; casting down imaginations, and every high thing that exalteth itself against the knowledge of God, and bringing into captivity every thought to the obedience of Christ.

What desires and dreams did I form in my youth that trouble me even now? Are there expectations that have been unfulfilled and left me feeling that I've failed, or I've missed God's best for my life? Have I failed to understand that God uses even disappointments for His glory and my own good? Can I identify disappointments in my life that turned out to be blessings or spared me from catastrophe or ruin?

Study the following Bible stories, considering how they might encourage and strengthen you.

Joseph was disappointed when his brothers sold him into slavery and when the baker forgot to mention him to Pharaoh—but God was at work using every disappointment for a purpose. God's timing was perfect.

Sarah was disappointed year after year when she did not become pregnant—but God prevented her from having children so He could work a greater plan in her life.

Mary and Martha were disappointed when their brother died—but God knew what He was doing and had a great purpose in allowing it to happen.

Parents of the man born blind were disappointed when they realized their baby could not see—but God had a wonderful plan for their child's life that required him to be blind.

Leah was disappointed that she was not as pretty or as popular as her sister Rachel—but God made Leah exactly as He had planned, and in Heaven, her disappointment turned to joy as she realized she was chosen to be in the lineage of Christ.

Naomi was disappointed when her husband and sons died—but God turned her disappointment into joy as He demonstrated His wisdom and ability to sustain her and bless her in her old age.

Lot's wife was disappointed when she was asked to leave her friends and home—but she could not trust God with her disappointment and lost the blessing she could have had.

Michal was disappointed that her plans did not materialize when her husband David lost his job in the palace and was forced to flee to the desert. She, too, could not trust God and wait on Him to turn things around *His* way. She forfeited the blessing she could have had.

Lesson 9

The Joy of Overcoming Impossible Circumstances

To comfort all that mourn, to appoint unto them that mourn in Zion, to give unto them beauty for ashes, the oil of joy for mourning, the garment of praise for the spirit of heaviness; that they might be called trees of righteousness, the planting of the LORD, that He might be glorified.
Isaiah 61:2b-3

My flesh and my heart faileth: but God is the strength of my heart, and my portion forever.
Psalm 73:26

Key Thoughts

COMFORT AND JOY
Focusing on God's purpose and future reward

SELF-PITY AND DEPRESSION
Focusing on the present discomfort and sorrow

Research Question: According to *Psalm 73:26*, what does the phrase *my flesh and my heart faileth* mean?

1. God invites us to call on Him when we are _____ _____ so that He can deliver us, and so we will happily _____ God. *Psalm 50:15*

2. A woman is happy when she _____ difficult circumstances and depends on the Lord for strength and help. *James 5:11*

3. When we go to the Lord for help in times of trouble, He holds us up. His words of _____ delight our soul. *Psalm 94:17-19*

4. In the same way a mother endures _____ because she is looking forward to the birth of her baby, we can endure trials when we look forward to God's rewards later. *John 16:21*

5. In the same way Jesus endured the cross because He looked forward to the _____ that was set before Him, we can endure our trials knowing they have an end and a purpose. *Hebrews 12:2*

*It is a mistake to suppose that men succeed through success; they much
more often succeed through failures.* —Samuel Smiles

Have you ever prayed, "But Lord, this isn't how I planned my life"? Or, "Lord, can you still use me?" Have you ever secretly wondered if you will feel normal again? Or, if your family life will ever be as happy as you once dreamed?

Have you, like Cinderella, ever felt trapped in a hopeless situation and wished you had a fairy godmother to rescue you? Perhaps you've cried in despair, knowing you need help—real help—not just sympathy. Perhaps your dreams of living happily ever after have been shattered. If so, God has great news for you! He not only understands heartaches, He also specializes in putting happy endings on stories just like yours!

When we find ourselves in an "impossible" situation, we want to be comforted, encouraged, and helped in practical ways. We want to know whether or not there's any hope for a miracle and whether or not our calamity means we have been given a life sentence of loss and sorrow. Although we may never say so out loud, we might fear God is condemning us for our failures or imagine He cannot possibly love us. We long to know a reason for our trouble and are often bewildered when God does not seem to show us why. As we begin to comprehend the bleakness of our situation, it might even seem as though every promise in the Bible is meant for someone else but me.

Seemingly impossible situations compel us to admit that our only hope is in God. We know that if He doesn't intervene on our behalf, our fate is all but sealed. In desperation we believe this moment in life is hopeless and we have nothing but God to hang on to and none but God who can deliver us. The familiar saying takes on more meaning: "When we come to the place where Christ is all we have, we will find that He is all we need." One thing is certain—when we realize God is all we have, we will seek Him diligently at the throne of grace.

We will either come boldly into God's presence, certain that we will obtain God's mercy and find the grace and help we so desperately need, or we will timidly approach God with fears of His rejection, having little confidence that He really hears or cares (*Hebrews 4:16*). What we know about God and how assured we are of His love will greatly determine how we respond to our trouble and how our story will end. For this reason, we need to become well grounded in our understanding of God's love and character and grow in our confidence to trust God's Word. Only then do we really learn how to let Jesus navigate us safely through a difficult and tempestuous storm.

We will begin this study by reviewing specific truths that help build our faith and bring us hope, comfort, and encouragement. Then we will tackle some of the more practical principles of handling an impossible situation Biblically.

Truth That Strengthens Faith

1. God delights in solving hard cases—yes, even yours. We acknowledge God's wisdom and truly glorify Him as we see Him bringing good out of evil and making beauty out of the ashes of our impossible circumstances.

2 Chronicles 16:9—For the eyes of the LORD run to and fro throughout the whole earth, to show himself strong in the behalf of them whose heart is perfect toward Him.

2. There is nothing (that means *nothing*) too hard for Him.

Jeremiah 32:17,27—Ah Lord GOD! Behold, thou hast made the heaven and the earth by Thy great power and stretched out Thy arm, and there is nothing too hard for Thee. Behold, I am the LORD, the God of all flesh: is there any thing too hard for Me?

3. There is NO circumstance or situation that is hopeless, no matter what failures have taken place in your past or how wronged you may have been.

2 Chronicles 30:9—For if ye turn again unto the LORD, your brethren and your children shall find compassion before them that lead them captive, so that they shall come again into this land: for the LORD your God is gracious and merciful, and will not turn away His face from you, if ye return unto Him.

4. God can enable you to be happy and content even in the midst of impossible circumstances.

Psalm 107:8,9,43—Oh that men would praise the LORD for His goodness, and for His wonderful works to the children of men! For He satisfieth the longing soul, and filleth the hungry soul with goodness. Whoso is wise, and will observe these things, even they shall understand the lovingkindness of the LORD.

5. God is eager to make your life a trophy of His grace, His power, and His love by *His* strength (not yours). But you must be willing to do it His way.

Isaiah 64:8—But now, O LORD, Thou art our father; we are the clay, and Thou our potter; and we all are the work of Thy hand.

6. There is no situation so impossible or so great that God will not provide all that is needed to meet its challenges and withstand its pain.

1 Corinthians 10:13—There hath no temptation [trial] taken you but such as is common to man; but God is faithful, [He cannot lie and will not let us down] Who will not suffer [allow] you to be tempted [tried] above that ye are able; but will with the temptation also make a way to escape, that ye may be able to bear it.

Consider the outcome of these impossible situations

1. Abraham failed in exercising faith numerous times, yet he ultimately became a man of faith, the father of the faithful, the friend of God.

2. Peter failed at courage and trusting God, yet ultimately become known as a man of boldness and trust in God.

3. Timothy grew up without a father, yet became a great, godly pastor.

4. Samuel was raised in a corrupt environment with Eli's wicked sons, yet he became a man of prayer and a great judge of Israel.

5. Joseph was the victim of gross injustice. He was motherless at a young age, and was raised in the ultimate "blended" family. Yet, Joseph learned to trust God and became a powerful, wise leader.

6. Daniel was separated from his family as a teenager and educated in a corrupt society, yet he remained faithful to God and lived an exemplary Christian life.

7. Rahab was a prostitute, yet later married one of Joshua's faithful spies, was praised as a woman of faith, and became the mother of Boaz and great grandmother of David. She has the honor of being listed in the genealogy of Christ.

8. Bathsheba committed adultery, yet became the mother of Solomon and was most likely the author of Proverbs 31, which is every Christian woman's pattern for womanly virtue.

Romans 8 Study

Finding comfort in times of trial begins with whom we know and what we know—what we are thoroughly convinced is true. Paul said, "[I] am persuaded that He is able to keep that which I have committed unto Him against that day" (*2 Timothy 1:12b*). Because Paul meticulously examined the evidence and became thoroughly acquainted with God's character, He came to the place where he could say, "I am persuaded; and I

NOTES

am convinced that God will do what He said He would do." Until we are thoroughly persuaded that God is able and willing to make our circumstances turn around for good…until we can confidently say like David, "I had fainted unless I had believed to see the good of the Lord in the land of the living…" none of God's promises bring lasting comfort or encouragement in times of great distress. We must be absolutely convinced that what God says is true for faith does not simply believe in what we want to believe, but believes in what God has clearly stated as truth.

Such confidence and faith only develops as we begin to know and understand the Word of God. "Faith cometh by hearing, and hearing by the Word of God." Faith is the outcome of "walking in the Spirit," living in harmony and fellowship with the Lord Jesus Christ. Faith is a God-given ability to believe and trust God at His word. Faith, as applied to salvation refers to "trust in" or "reliance upon" all Christ's claims about Himself, as well as the Gospel message itself. Faith is trust in the person of the Lord Jesus Christ, in all He taught and in all He did at Calvary on our behalf, which results in submission to Him and to His message. Faith involves the heart, which implies that faith is something that affects our whole being, including our thoughts, our emotions, and our will. Faith always rests in the Word of God—God's testimony, His promises, and His character. Those who refuse to believe that God can do a work in the face of the impossible are in error because, like the Pharisees, they do not know the Scriptures or the power of God.

Because we know that God cannot lie, we know that God can be trusted. Faith does not require an understanding of the purpose, how, when, or where that God will fulfill what He has promised, but quietly depends and waits on God to do what He has promised regardless of what seemingly impossible obstacles or hardships appear to stand in the way. Whether we have much faith, or are among those with little faith, we have faith nonetheless. What love and kindness to be assured by Jesus that even the littlest faith is enough to "move mountains." No Christian is left out—all are able to exercise enough faith to see the impossible accomplished. (For further study: *John 3:36; John 5:24; John 16:27, 33; Hebrews 12:2*)

One of the most comforting and well known passages of Scripture begins by saying, "And we *know*…." *Romans 8:28* is a sparkling ray of sunshine and hope in the darkest of trials. This verse is a precious promise that only a child of God can claim and find comfort in. It says, "And we know that all things work together for good to them that love God, to them who are the called according to his purpose." The little phrase "all things" takes in every catastrophe, every failure, every disappointment, every injustice, and every event both good and bad that comes into a believer's life. There are no exceptions for the Bible does not say, "some things." The promise firmly asserts that

God causes *all things* to work out for good. God doesn't spare us from all things, but He turns every single one around to accomplish good. What Satan and others mean for evil, God miraculously and skillfully overrules in the lives of His children.

While we often quote *Romans 8:28*, we seldom take the time to examine the preceding or following verses. The eighth chapter of Romans begins with an equally great promise that provides wonderful comfort in times of adversity. This chapter begins by answering one of the most common fears believers express in times of trial, *"Is God condemning me?"* God's answer to us is, "There is therefore now no condemnation to those which are in Christ Jesus." God does not condemn those who are forgiven and washed by the blood of Christ. He corrects as a father does his child, but He does not punish or condemn. When trouble comes into our life, the trial is not punishment or retribution for sin. Jesus took our punishment for us on the cruel cross of Calvary. We may suffer the consequences of our sinful choices, and we may suffer under the hand of God's correction that is administered for our good and for our future joy, but we are never corrected with anger or contempt and are never rejected, condemned, or destroyed.

In verse *31* through *39* of *Romans 8*, Paul addresses many of the most common questions and fears that tenderhearted believers express when unexplained trials come their way. The first question usually asked is, "why?" Verse *29* tells us why we suffer all things—because God is using them to conform us to be like Christ. Paul then goes on to answer the common fear of rejection in verse *31*, "What shall we then say to these things? If God be for us, who can be against us?" Paul assures us that since God is for us, no one who rises up against us can prevail. He then goes on to remind us that even Jesus was not spared the "all things" that come into a life. God loved His Son with a love we cannot begin to comprehend, yet He allowed Him to suffer so that we could be spared. God did not allow Jesus to be afflicted because He was rejecting or condemning Him. He allowed the affliction because it had a purpose and was the only way He could accomplish our redemption.

Verse *33* is a wonderful response to the common feelings of guilt that often plague believers going through a particularly difficult trial. Paul assures the believer by asking the question, "Who shall lay anything to the charge of God's elect? It is God that justifieth." Paul is saying that God has completely forgiven and justified the believer and there is not *anything* that can be held against him. Certainly the "all things" that come into his life are not punishment for his sins. Verse 34 goes on to ask, "Who is he that condemneth? It is Christ that died, yea rather, that is risen again, who is even at the right hand of God, who also maketh intercession for us."

NOTES

No one, not even our self, can condemn one whom God has made righteous by His blood. Because we are justified and given the privileges of God's children, we need only honestly confess our sin to our Heavenly Father to restore fellowship broken by sin. He promises, "If we walk in the light as He is in the light, we have fellowship one with another, and the blood of Jesus Christ His Son, cleanseth us from all sin" (1 John 1:7). Our standing with God does not depend on our own righteousness—our position depends only upon the righteousness that is given to us by faith in Christ.

Finally, Paul addresses the common fear that suffering is an indication that God does not love us. He begins by saying, "Who shall separate us from the love of Christ? Shall tribulation, or distress, or persecution, or famine, or nakedness, or peril, or sword?" Paul is speaking as much from his own experience as from what he knows the Scripture to say, for he has experienced each of these things. He reminds believers that every believer experiences injustice and seemingly senseless trials for the cause of Christ, including himself. This wouldn't be a comforting thought if it were not for the next statement. "Nay, in all these things we are more than conquerors through him that loved us." We aren't just given victory over trials; we are *more* than conquerors. In other words, our trials not only fail to destroy us, they are made to work out for good and further the cause of Christ.

Paul ends the chapter by asserting once again that he is thoroughly persuaded....he *knows*... "that neither death, nor life, nor angels, nor principalities, nor powers, nor things present, nor things to come, nor height, nor depth, nor any other creature shall be able to separate us from the love of God which is in Christ Jesus our Lord."

Truths That Comfort and Encourage Our Heart

1. Remember that God loves His children with a love that will never end and can never be destroyed. His love for us is dependent upon His own character, not ours. He loves us simply because we are His.

Jeremiah 31:3—The LORD hath appeared of old unto me, saying, Yea, I have loved thee with an everlasting love: therefore with lovingkindness have I drawn thee.

Ephesians 2:4-7—But God, Who is rich in mercy, for His great love wherewith He loved us, even when we were dead in sins, hath quickened us together with Christ, (by grace ye are saved;) and hath raised us up together, and made us sit together in heavenly places in Christ Jesus; that in the ages to come He might show the exceeding riches of His grace in His kindness toward us through Christ Jesus.

Page 108

2. Remember that the battle is fought primarily in our minds. The way we think and believe will determine the way we act and the way we feel.

2 Corinthians 10:4-5—(For the weapons of our warfare are not carnal, but mighty through God to the pulling down of strong holds;) casting down imaginations, and every high thing that exalteth itself against the knowledge of God, and bringing into captivity every thought to the obedience of Christ.

3. Remember that suffering caused by sin does not mean God has not forgiven us. Though we fall and are down for a moment, God picks us up again and prevents us from being utterly destroyed.

1 John 1:8-9—If we say that we have no sin, we deceive ourselves, and the truth is not in us. If we confess our sins, He is faithful and just to forgive us our sins, and to cleanse us from all unrighteousness.

Psalm 37:23-24—The steps of a good man are ordered by the Lord; and he delighteth in His way. Though he fall, he shall not be utterly cast down, for the Lord upholdeth him with His hand.

In Case of Emergency....

Call upon the Lord! Prayer is a crucial first step when trials come because it is the God-ordained means of calling upon God and eliciting His response. God has a specific order—first we step out in faith and call upon our God, then He answers and delivers us from trouble (*Psalm 50:15*). Call upon God in prayer, and then follow the lead of the Holy Spirit as He directs you through God's Word. Depend on Him to give direction as the situation unfolds. Remember, in the fear of the Lord is strong confidence; and His children shall have a place of refuge (*Proverbs 14:26*). We are not to behave as though we are in this trial alone or as if the Captain of the host is not leading the way into battle.

When a situation looks absolutely impossible, it is God's glory to intervene on behalf of His children and turn the situation around in miraculous or unexpected ways. This is because only then are we able to clearly see His hand of mercy and know that it was not by our own strength or wisdom that we were delivered, but by His strength and wisdom. When an army that far outnumbered King Asa surrounded King Asa and his men, King Asa realized he didn't have a chance—humanly speaking that is. The situation was impossible, and he didn't have to think twice about how hopeless and utterly defeated he was.

King Asa was not among the unbelievers who would have given up hope or tried to muster up strength within himself. In this crisis He did not depend on his own wisdom or ability to reason things out and find a solution. When he saw what he was up against, King Asa immediately cried out to the Lord on the spot and said, "Lord, it is nothing with Thee to help whether with many or with them that have no power; help us O Lord our God; for we rest on Thee, and in Thy name we go against this multitude. O Lord, Thou art our God; let not man prevail against Thee" (*2 Chronicles 14:11*).

King Asa knew he was inadequate, but thankfully, he also knew God was more than adequate to see him through, no matter what the odds of defeat were. Next we see the result of his faith in God and his lack of faith in himself. The following verse says, "So the Lord smote the Ethiopians before Asa and before Judah; and the Ethiopians fled." Notice who did the smiting? It was the Lord Himself.

When the Lord is our helper, we need not fear what man can do to us (*Hebrews 13:6*). We are able to respond confidently to every crisis by calling upon God and putting our trust in Him. We have this boldness, not because in and of ourselves we are strong or confident in our abilities, but because we have a sovereign God who goes into battle with us and does not leave us helpless or without resources in Him. "We have boldness and access with confidence by the faith of him" (*Ephesians 3:12*).

When facing "the impossible," consider these cautions:

1. **Avoid making a quick judgment.** Suspend drawing conclusions until you have complete information; know that God's way of dealing with a situation may not be what seems logical to us. God says in *Isaiah 55:8-9*, "For My thoughts are not your thoughts, neither are your ways My ways, saith the LORD. For as the heavens are higher than the earth, so are My ways higher than your ways, and My thoughts than your thoughts."

2. **Be certain that every response and every solution you choose is both ethical and Biblical.** This is essential if you desire God's blessing. If your solution does not pass this criterion, it must be rejected. God *always* prepares a way of escape in every trial, and His escape is *never* unbiblical or unethical in any way. You may need to be willing to make a significant investment of time and effort to deal with a problem righteously. Few crisis situations are quick and easy to resolve. In fact, some require very long-term endurance and commitment.

3. **Concentrate on dealing with your situation one step at a time, as this is the way God walks with us through a trial.** Sometimes we won't know exactly what steps we need to take immediately or how the problem will gradually unfold. We will need to discipline ourselves to take one day and one problem at a time without stretching our necks to see what is at the end of a very winding road. We can only see one bend at a time, so it is futile to waste any effort wondering what lies several miles of bends ahead. Rest assured that God gives us exactly what we need to know to take the next step and respond today. Then as we round that corner, He prepares us to face the next. Remember that God did not teach us to pray for our monthly bread—He taught us to pray for our daily bread. He doesn't give us tomorrow's grace, for tomorrow isn't here. He gives us today's grace, because today's grace is what we need. Jesus told us not to worry about tomorrow, because tomorrow will have enough challenges of its own. He knows that the trials we face in one day are enough to handle.

4. **Focus on the good kinds of outcome that will come out of the crisis, not on the pain of the crisis itself.** Although we don't know at the start how we are going to get where God wants us to go, we do know we will get there if we walk along with Him day by day. The first book of Peter was written to suffering believers who faced horrendous crisis problems. Peter could not tell them how God would specifically sustain each of them or where God would lead each one. What He could tell them about the future was that their present suffering had a great reward, both in this life and in the next. Through Scripture, He shows them that there is a reason behind suffering, that there is grace and strength in the midst of it, and that there is a reward ahead of the suffering. We might not know the road, but we do know the destination. Throughout the book of Peter, suffering believers are urged to look up, not within, to look forward to the purpose and future rewards, not at the present suffering. We, as well as they, need to be reminded to make wise decisions today that will not be regretted around the bend tomorrow.

You will become encouraged and uplifted as you commit yourself to live a life of obedience to God, knowing God and God alone is able to make "beauty out of ashes" in your life *(Psalm 143:10; Isaiah 61:3)*.

When facing "the impossible," ask yourself the following questions:

- Have I done all God wants me to do concerning the problem?
- Have I made a commitment to do the right thing, rather than the easiest thing, because I know that in the end, right is always best?

- Am I violating any Scriptural command or principle in the way I'm trying to solve my problem? For example, people often stop tithing or cheat on taxes to get out of debt. Sometimes women divorce a difficult husband, live with a man instead of insisting on marriage, or date an unsaved man instead of waiting on God and doing right. Commonly, young mothers choose to leave small children when things get tight rather than find other ways to supplement the family income. Many will use a credit card instead of depending on God to meet their need or give them grace to live within their budget. So often people *choose success* and *instant relief* rather than doing as Moses and choosing the right way instead of the easy or "logical" way. Read *Hebrews 12:23-29* before you rationalize your method of solving your problem!

- Am I willing to obey Christ, even if it takes time before I am rewarded and see God's blessing unfold?

- Am I willing to entrust my case completely to Christ and look to Him alone to turn the situation around as He desires?

Scriptures that help us learn to trust God

Proverbs 3:5—Trust in the LORD with all thine heart; and lean not unto thine own understanding.

Psalm 18:30-33—As for God, His way is perfect; the Word of the Lord is tried; He is a buckler to all those that trust in Him. For Who is God save the Lord? Or, Who is a rock save our God? It is God that girdeth me with strength, and maketh my way perfect. He maketh my feet like hinds' feet, and setteth me upon my high places.

Psalm 34:8—O taste and see that the Lord is good: blessed is the man that trusteth in Him. O fear the Lord, ye His saints; for there is no want to them that fear Him.

Every trial, problem, sorrow, and failure, can be turned to joy if we know our God, depend on His faithfulness, His love, and His promises. Our joy is not in the trial itself, but in knowing the end results.

Hebrews 12:2a—Looking unto Jesus the author and finisher of our faith; who for the joy that was set before Him endured the cross.

Isaiah 26:3—Thou wilt keep him in perfect peace, whose mind is stayed on Thee; because he trusteth in Thee.

Romans 5:1—Therefore being justified by faith, we have peace with God through our Lord Jesus Christ, by whom also we have access by faith into this grace wherein we stand, and rejoice in hope of the glory of God.

John 16:33a—These things I have spoken unto you, that in me ye might have peace.

Lesson 10

The Joy of Understanding Anger

Thou shalt not hate thy brother in thine heart: thou shalt in any wise rebuke thy neighbor, and not suffer sin upon him. Thou shalt not avenge, nor bear any grudge against the children of thy people, but thou shalt love thy neighbor as thyself: I am the LORD.
Leviticus 19:17-18

Wherefore, my beloved brethren, let every man be swift to hear, slow to speak, slow to wrath: for the wrath of man worketh not the righteousness of God.
James 1:19-20

Key Thoughts

A Loving Heart
Comes by yielding personal rights and demonstrating love for others

An Angry Heart
Comes by having selfish demands and intolerance for others

Research Question: According to *Ephesians 4:26*, what does the phrase *be angry and sin not* mean?

1. Women who control their _____ are joyful. *Proverbs 15:23*

2. When a woman _____, she has joy and peace. *Romans 15:13*

3. A woman must make a deliberate decision to be _____. *Psalm 104:34*

4. A woman who cultivates meekness (humility) will increase her _____. *Isaiah 29:19*

5. Knowing _____ _____ of life makes women joyful. *Acts 2:28*

6. A woman who has the _____ _____ _____ _____ will become satisfied. *Proverbs 19:23*

7. When a woman _____ to the Lord, she is happy. *Psalm 71:23*

Quarrels would not last long if the fault was only on one side. —La Rochefoucauld

Righteous and Sinful Anger

Where, asks James, does anger and fighting among people originate? What causes such strife? The answer is swift and simple and not always what we want to hear. The problem lies within us, he replies, not without (*James 4:1*). The Bible clearly teaches that anger originates in our corrupted human nature and is the outward manifestation of inward self-motivated desires. But, you might object, what about righteous anger? And what about anger as an emotion? Surely it can't be wrong or selfish to experience the emotion of anger when someone has just wronged you or treated you with cruelty! Wouldn't expressions of anger be justified in such cases?

Yes, there is such a thing as righteous anger; and yes, anger can be an appropriate emotion. In the vast majority of cases, however, expressed anger is clearly sinful. This sinful expression isn't something people readily want to admit. Quite frankly, admitting sin goes against our human nature. Even Christians are not always willing to evaluate their angry reactions in light of God's Word or use Biblical criteria to determine whether they are expressing righteous or unrighteous (sinful) anger.

Most people want to excuse, justify, or redefine what God wants His children to face and conquer by His power and grace. Honest self-evaluation requires an enormous amount of courage, humility and God-given grace. It is not for the fainthearted or shortsighted! Those who have spiritual ears to hear and eyes to see will gladly humble themselves before God with a willingness to reject their own reasoning and lean instead on God's. According to *James 4:6*, these will discover God's enabling grace and mercy to conquer sinful anger. On the other hand, those who depend on their own human reasoning and determination will discover they cannot obtain God's overcoming power because God resists [is opposed to] the proud. No amount of pleading will elicit God's help until the heart is humbled and dependent on Christ alone.

Before we discuss the roots of anger in light of God's Word, let's clarify the difference between righteous and sinful anger. The Bible distinguishes righteous anger as anger on behalf of others. Righteous anger is anger that imitates God's anger, which is always controlled and with purpose. Righteous anger is not accompanied by hatred, malice, or resentment; it is not selfish, but expresses care and concern. The purpose of righteous anger is to correct or curtail destructive behavior, never to break relationships. God's anger is directed at injustice or willful disobedience. Righteous anger is always expressed on behalf of another who is oppressed, abused, or betrayed.

Man's anger, in contrast, is usually uncontrolled and without patience; it is characterized by hatred, malice, resentment, and selfishness. Sometimes man's anger is used as an expression of indignation. It destroys individuals, is often an expression of revenge, and is intended to hurt others. Man's anger is an expression directed toward those who hurt or violate us. Sinful anger always is a reaction to offenses against oneself. Throughout the centuries, man's sinful anger has left a trail of destruction more devastating than drugs or any natural disaster. Nothing has destroyed more relationships and families, caused more children to rebel, or discouraged more Christians than anger. Nothing has destroyed churches, governments, nations, organizations, or partnerships quite like anger. Anger is deadly. No wonder Jesus connected anger with hatred and murder. Anger does kill and destroy.

Righteous anger is directed toward the same things, in the same way, and for the same motives as God's anger. Even when anger is a righteous response, it is to be controlled and kept in its proper place, lest it destroy others and us by turning into bitterness. We are never allowed freedom to take vengeance on anyone out of *righteous anger*, but are to trust God to be God and to execute proper vengeance in His time. We are permitted to use the righteous and just means God has provided for us to use in dealing with offenders and offenses, not our own human methods. These God-given means may include the use of law enforcement, the court system, church discipline, godly confrontation and appeal, etc. Apart from these, we are commanded to entrust our case to Him who has both the power and right to execute justice. Even in all these actions, we are never to be driven by hateful anger, or delight in seeing our enemy suffer.

The emotion of anger is not sinful; the motivations and expressions of our angry emotions are sinful. For example, one might "rejoice" when his enemy falls in some way. The emotion of joy isn't sinful—it *is* the reason behind the emotion that God condemns in *Proverbs 24:17*. In Ephesians 4:26 Paul tells us, "Be ye angry, and sin not; let not the sun go down upon your wrath; neither give place to the devil." Paul is acknowledging the emotion of anger as a part of our human experience. Even so, he admonishes us not to express the emotion of anger in sinful ways (no matter how terribly we have been wronged) and not to leave anger unresolved. He tells us in *Romans 12:18*, "If it be possible, as much as lieth in you, live peaceably with all men." To the extent we are able, we must strive for peace and actively pursue reconciliation with others. When we ignore this admonishment and fail to resolve problems and seek peace on God's terms, we give the devil a foothold into our lives and pave the way for destruction.

The Origin of Anger

The Bible clearly teaches that all sinful anger originates in our corrupted human nature and is the outward manifestation of inward, self-motivated desires. Adverse circumstances and people may cause the anger of the heart to surface, but they do not cause the anger in the heart. We like to say, "Such and such or so and so *MADE* me angry," as if such and such or so and so held a gun to our heads and forced us to react in anger. While circumstances may indeed provoke strong emotion in us, our individual *interpretation* of circumstances and our own sinful desires and choices ultimately incite sinful anger. The Bible tells us that anger arises out of our lust [selfish desires] that war in our members [within us] (*James 4:1*). When our hearts are filled with "I want," "I need," and "I deserve," sinful anger is lurking at the door.

We will react in anger when our desires become something we believe we are entitled to and they are in some way withheld from us. The desire is not necessarily wrong—it is the place of importance we give that desire and whether we are willing to sin in order to get it that is wrong. A desire that has become a requirement for our happiness or a demand of any kind completely leaves God out of the equation. The order of importance fails to take into consideration the fact that God has sovereignly ordained us to live in an imperfect world and expects us to learn to respond to it by submitting to God's ways and will. Anger is essentially an expression of our heart that says, "I don't like what has just happened, and I am extremely unhappy about it." Our feelings and our wants become the prime issue at the moment we express sinful anger—our thoughts aren't focused on God's work in the matter, what He wants to accomplish or how He wants us to respond to disappointment, injustice, the sinful behavior of others or adversities common to this life. Instead, lightening quick thoughts along the lines of "he should" or "he shouldn't" or "how dare he" invariably take center stage in our minds and immediately precede expressions of anger.

James describes the futile attempts of angry people to get what they want in verse two of chapter four. "Ye lust, and have not; ye kill, and desire to have, and cannot obtain; ye fight and war, yet ye have not, because ye ask not. Ye ask, and receive not, because ye ask amiss, that ye may consume it upon your lusts." Angry people want life on their own terms, without inconveniences, disappointments, or suffering of any kind. They passionately want their own way, whatever that way is, and they will attempt to circumvent God, or sin, in order to get their way. They are not willing to see God in every situation of life, nor are they willing to wait patiently for Him to work on their behalf. Even if they pray for whatever it is they desire, they have only their own desires in mind. They are like Martha who came to Jesus asking Him to make Mary get up and help. Angry people do not want what Jesus wants, and they

NOTES

NOTES

have no intention of giving up their desires for His. They want Him to side with them and cater to their selfish demands. When Jesus isn't manipulated or bullied into giving them what they ask for, they are all the more agitated or discouraged.

Angry behavior as we have described reveals a prideful desire to govern one's own life. At its roots, anger is a desire to exalt and worship self and a refusal to yield to the authority and Lordship of Christ. This is why James goes on to address angry people as spiritual adulterers who think and behave in the same way the world does. To become angry at what God allows or disallows is to accuse and reject God Himself. It is the epitome of pride because it puts self in God's place and gives to one's self the prerogatives and rights that only God can have. The angry and prideful heart depends on itself to decide what is good and bad, what should or shouldn't happen or how others are to behave.

The reasoning of a sinful human heart propels the heart to reject what God may want and embrace, and instead embrace what *it* wants. This is why Biblical accounts of incidents involving anger are invariably connected in some way to pride. The two are inseparable twins. Pride ignores God and focuses instead on one's perceived purity and rights. Humility, in contrast, bows to God's sovereignty and sees God as holy and pure, and sees self as frail and undeserving of the least of God's favor. Humility does not clench a fist around its rights making God pry loose one finger at a time. Rather, a humble spirit willingly opens its hand to God with childlike trust. Humility recognizes God's wisdom and power in contrast with our human ignorance and weakness, His perfection and authority with our imperfection and lowliness, and His faithfulness and provision with our unfaithfulness and dependence on Him for everything.

In James, verse six and seven ties all the preceding verses in chapter four together and draws a conclusion that also happens to be the greatest antidote to anger. It says, "God resisteth [is opposed to] the proud, but giveth grace [unmerited favor, desire and ability to do God's will] to the humble. Submit yourselves therefore to God. Resist the devil, and he will flee from you." It is possible to control anger by human efforts provided the motivation is strong enough, but none can ever conquer anger without submitting their heart and life wholly to God. Anger and pride are the hallmark of Satan. He thrives and perpetuates on these sinful twins by exploiting man's selfish tendencies for his own sinful purpose and goals. Man cannot win this spiritual battle against the world, the flesh, and the devil by fighting in worldly ways or exerting his own willpower and determination. We succeed in fighting our sinful nature and the wiles of the devil by bowing our will to God and submitting wholly to Christ alone. To submit to God is to resist the devil. *James 4:10* records, "Humble yourselves in the sight of the Lord, and He shall lift you up." Humility, then, is the cornerstone truth that will lead to true freedom from anger.

The Expression of Anger

Anger is expressed in many ways besides the common blowing up or speaking hatefully. While anger commonly takes the form of loud outrage, verbal attacks, throwing objects, or slamming a door, anger is expressed just as easily by crying, clamming up, refusing to cooperate with others, or sulking. Some resort to physical violence such as hitting, slapping, or kicking when a person or thing gets in the way or displeases. Others use sarcasm, excessive teasing, or biting humor to vent their buried anger. Many expressions of hostility and anger are easily recognizable—others are not. Those who are inwardly and quietly seething with anger may not even recognize it in themselves. Such people typically learn to use words that are often masked expressions of anger. These include "I'm annoyed." "I'm irritated." "I'm fed up." "I'm hurt." "I'm frustrated." In all honesty, words such as these might more accurately be replaced with, "I'm angry."

Some people are able to keep their anger so well hidden that others never so much as suspect a problem with anger. The single most difficult aspect of identifying and conquering anger is coming to a place where there is a willingness to face, admit, and Biblically deal with one's own sins in the matter. Angry people tend to convince themselves (and others) that their anger and related problems are a direct result of circumstances they did not bring about, or a result of other people in their life who have not dealt with them in ways they believe they deserve. Attempts to justify or excuse anger contribute to this self-deception and keep an angry person in bondage to the sin of anger. Anger always betrays our belief that we have a right to expect someone or something to fulfill our desires; and when they don't, flaring up in obvious or hurtful ways is viewed as justifiable, if not reasonable.

An orange tree produces oranges because it is an orange tree. In the same way, we are sinful people that produce sin because we are sinners. If we control the environment of the orange tree by depriving it of light or nutrients, it may not produce oranges—but it is still an orange tree. All we have to do to prove the tree's identity is expose the tree to normal conditions favorable to orange trees so that it will once again produce oranges. People may not produce sin when there is no provocation; however, introduce financial pressure, a disagreeable neighbor, a lack of sleep, or unjust treatment and see what happens. That which is really deep inside the heart will rise to the surface in a split second reaction. The Bible tells us, "For out of the heart proceed evil thoughts, murders, adulteries, fornications, thefts, false witness, blasphemies..." (*Matthew 15:19*).

People like to imagine they are fairly righteous and good—that only certain conditions provoke them to be unnaturally sinful. The truth is that adverse circumstances simply reveal what we really are inside and convince us that God is correct in the way He assesses our sinful condition. Paul provides an unflattering picture of our sinful human heart apart from the changing grace of God in *Romans 3:11-18*. He follows it by saying, "Now we know that what things soever the law saith, it saith to them who are under the law: that every mouth may be stopped, and all the world may become guilty before God." Before we can understand our need of salvation and/or receive God's wonderful cleansing power, we must first face the unpleasant truth that our words and actions really do reveal the true condition of our heart.

Following is a list of questions that will assist you in examining and confronting your own tendencies to hide or justify anger. Use it as a self-evaluation to provoke yourself to be honest and humble as you seek the Lord's direction in your Christian growth. As you progress in this study, you should be increasingly more able to see the connection between your answers and the specific areas in your life that are in need of God's transforming change.

Recognizing Anger Worksheet

1. What frustrates me?

2. What lingering disappointments do I have?

3. What/who discourages me?

4. What irritates/bugs me?

5. What injustices bother me?

6. What fears trouble me?

7. Am I manifesting physical expressions of anger such as chronic tenseness, fatigue, recurring headaches, unexplained gastrointestinal disorders, chronic respiratory disorders, circulatory disorders, unexplained heart palpitations or chest pain?
   _____ Often   _____ Sometimes   _____ Seldom   _____ Not at all

8. Is the thought of being angry unacceptable or threatening to me?
   _____ Often   _____ Sometimes   _____ Seldom   _____ Not at all

9. Do I often feel sad, unhappy, fed up, annoyed, hurt, or harassed?
   _____ Often   _____ Sometimes   _____ Seldom   _____ Not at all

10. Do I often talk about being frustrated, disappointed, or ready to explode?
    _____ Often   _____ Sometimes   _____ Seldom   _____ Not at all

11. When I am confronted, do I quickly shift the blame to someone else, or do I point out other people who are doing the same thing or something I believe is worse?
    _____ Often   _____ Sometimes   _____ Seldom   _____ Not at all

12. Is admitting fault painful or difficult for me?
    _____ Often   _____ Sometimes   _____ Seldom   _____ Not at all

13. Am I keenly aware of the faults of others or find certain people impossible to be with?
    _____ Often   _____ Sometimes   _____ Seldom   _____ Not at all

14. Is the thought of failure or not living up to a standard I've set for myself something that produces anxiety in my life?
    _____ Often   _____ Sometimes   _____ Seldom   _____ Not at all

15. Do I quickly notice when other people fail to live up to standards and convictions that I believe are important?   _____ Often   _____ Sometimes   _____ Seldom   _____ Not at all

Following are several explanations and passages of Scripture that will assist you in developing a Biblical understanding of anger. Study each one as you seek to find personal applications and life-guiding principles. On a 3x5 card, copy each verse that you find enlightening or helpful. Write a personal application and principle to live by on the back of each card. Read your cards often until the Scriptures are firmly lodged in your heart and become an integrated truth in your life.

Anger Begins in the Mind

Leviticus 19:17-18—Thou shalt not hate thy brother in thine heart: thou shalt in any wise rebuke thy neighbour, and not suffer sin upon him. Thou shalt not avenge, nor bear any grudge against the children of thy people, but thou shalt love thy neighbour as thyself: I am the LORD.

Ephesians 2:3—Among whom also we all had our conversation [behavior] in times past in the lusts of our flesh, fulfilling the desires of the flesh and of the mind; and were by nature the children of wrath, even as others.

Notice how God draws our attention to the significance of our private thought life in relation to anger. In *Leviticus 19*, God gives specific instructions that will prevent sinful expressions of anger. First and foremost, we are reminded that God forbids us to harbor hatred toward another in our hearts (minds). He instructs us to confront problems directly and honestly, going to one who sins against us for the purpose of helping him see his offense. Next, God forbids us to take matters into our own hands by avenging ourselves or retaliating, and forbids us from harboring any kind of grudge against others. Finally, God commands us to love our neighbor in the same way we naturally love ourselves. To merely stop holding a grudge or to ignore a sin is not enough.

God's way is to put off sinful behavior and actively and deliberately choose to put on its righteous counterpart, which in this case is love.

Anger is to be Controlled / Mastered

Proverbs 16:32—He that is slow to anger is better than the mighty; and he that ruleth his spirit than he that taketh a city.

Proverbs 25:28—He that hath no rule over his own spirit is like a city that is broken down, and without walls.

Paul tells us that he has to work at disciplining himself. In *1 Corinthians 9:27* we read, "But I keep under my body, and bring it into subjection." Later he tells us how to win our battles with the flesh: "Casting down imaginations [reasonings], and every high thing that exalteth itelf against the knowledge of God, and bringing into captivity every thought to the obedience of Christ" *(2 Corinthians 10:5)*. Bringing ourselves under subjection to Christ requires a deliberate choice to discipline ourselves for that purpose. Successful people work hard to accomplish their goals. Athletes, soldiers, and professionals of all kinds spend painstaking efforts to develop their particular proficiency. The Christian life is a disciplined life, intended to reap the joys and privileges of victory. While the world admires the accomplishments of its heroes, Heaven recognizes the true greatness of a Christian who has learned to govern his own inner spirit and emotions through God's strength and power.

God compares the Christian who fails to build up the protective walls of discipline around his life with an ancient city that neglected to build and repair protective walls around it. Such carelessness left the city open to the easy access and destruction of the enemy. In the same way, the Christian who does not work hard to rule his spirit leaves himself open to destructive enemies that will take advantage of such an easy entrance into his life.

Venting anger by beating a pillow, screaming, or swearing does not resolve a problem or bring the peace that believers seek. Victory is found in learning to harness anger's energy and redirecting it to solve problems in tangible and Biblically consistent ways.

Anger Never Accomplishes God's Will, is Not Blessed of God

James 1:19-22—Wherefore, my beloved brethren, let every man be swift to hear, slow to speak, slow to wrath: for the wrath of man worketh not the righteousness of God. Wherefore lay apart all filthiness and superfluity of naughtiness, and receive with meekness the engrafted word, which is able to save your souls. But be ye doers of the word, and not hearers only, deceiving your own selves.

Anger NEVER accomplishes God's will and is NEVER blessed by God. Anger does *not* produce the righteousness of God. It does *not* change people. It does *not* build up homes or churches or organizations or governments. It only tears down and destroys. Anger may intimidate and stop behavior, but it can never change another person's heart or behavior.

God gives a solemn warning to women when He says in Proverbs 14:1 "Every wise woman buildeth her house: but the foolish plucketh it down with her hands." The *tearing down* referred to in this passage isn't referring to a physical house being pulled apart brick by brick. God is talking about the foolish woman who tears down people and relationships within her home in an effort to control, rather than build up. To lash out at others with cruel words and cutting accusations is a wicked and dangerous thing, for words can never, never be taken back. Very often, though they are later regretted and cried over with bitter tears; the damage they brought remains, and relationships are never restored to what they could have been.

Anger is a Work of the Sinful Flesh, the Mark of an Immature Believer

Proverbs 14:17—He that is soon angry dealeth foolishly: and a man of wicked devices is hated.

James 3:13-17—Who *is* a wise man and endued with knowledge among you? Let him show out of a good conversation [behavior] his works with meekness [humility] of wisdom. But if ye have bitter envying and strife in your hearts, glory not, and lie not against the truth. This wisdom descendeth not from above, but *is* earthly, sensual, devilish. For where envying and strife *is*, there *is* confusion and every evil work. But the wisdom that is from above is first pure, then peaceable, gentle, *and* easy to be intreated, full of mercy and good fruits, without partiality, and without hypocrisy.

Galatians 5:19-21—Now the works of the flesh are manifest, which are these; adultery, fornication, uncleanness, lasciviousness, idolatry, witchcraft, hatred, variance, emulations, wrath, strife, seditions, heresies, envyings, murders, drunkenness, revelings, and such like.

The unbeliever is characterized by anger, according to *Ephesians 2:3*. Before salvation we are, by nature, the children of wrath. When a sinner repents and turns to God for forgiveness, God gives him a new inner nature, one like His own. The old nature dies and the new nature brings everything in life into a new perspective. This new perspective and awareness of one's freedom from the penalty and guilt of sin dispels anger. Nevertheless, the new Christian nature still lives in the same mortal body that is contaminated by the effects of sin.

While sin no longer has dominion over a believer or keeps him locked in an escape-proof box, sin is still an enemy out to destroy him. There is wonderful hope for the child of God because God gives His children everything they need to overcome sin's control. As they grow in their knowledge of Christ and learn how to appropriate truth into their life, anger is chipped away. A supernatural spirit of gentleness, patience and love characterizes the maturing believer. This is called the "fruit of the Spirit" and is the natural byproduct of one who lives his life in harmony with God's Word. The fruit of God's Spirit is the Christ likeness that God desires for every believer. Unlike anger, which comes naturally to human beings, the fruit of God's Spirit does not.

The more immature we are spiritually, the more our reactions will look like the world's reactions. The more mature we are spiritually, the more our instantaneous reactions will pattern those of our Lord Jesus Christ. Peter asks, "For what glory is it, if, when ye be buffeted for your faults, ye shall take it patiently? But if, when ye do well, and suffer for it, ye take it patiently, this is acceptable with God. For even hereunto were ye called: because Christ also suffered for us, leaving us an example, that ye should follow His steps." If you were mistreated, as Jesus was the day He was crucified, would you have been able to accept it quietly without cursing under your breath or hating your persecutors? One of the most incredible things about Jesus' crucifixion is the fact that in spite of all the gross injustice, humiliation, and cruelty leveled against Him, He "did no sin, neither was guile found in His mouth: who when He was reviled, reviled not again; when He suffered, He threatened not; but committed Himself to Him that judgeth righteously" (*I Peter 2:20-24*). This is the mark of miraculous love and forgiveness which is a natural part of God's nature, not our own.

Sinful Anger is a Result of Our Proud Self-Will

Proverbs 13:10a—Only by pride cometh contention.

James 4:1-3—From whence *come* wars and fightings among you? *Come they* not hence, *even* of your lusts that war in your members? Ye lust, and have not: ye kill, and desire to have, and cannot obtain: ye fight and war, yet ye have not, because ye ask not. Ye ask, and receive not, because ye ask amiss, that ye may consume *it* upon your lusts."

James 4:5-8—Do ye think that the Scripture saith in vain, The spirit that dwelleth in us lusteth to envy? But He giveth more grace. Wherefore He saith, God resisteth the proud, but giveth grace unto the humble. Submit yourselves therefore to God. Resist the devil, and he will flee from you. Draw nigh to God, and He will draw nigh to you. Cleanse *your* hands, *ye* sinners; and purify *your* hearts, *ye* double minded.

Anger and pride are mentioned in the same context in Scripture almost invariably. The Bible teaches us that contention *always* stems from pride (self-interest). Love and forgiveness, (which is the righteous counterpart to anger), stems from self-denial and a correct estimation of self (undeserving of God's love and forgiveness, possessing a deceitful and wicked heart that must always be under subjection to God's authority and never trusted, etc.). Contempt for others stems, not from *their* failures or sins, but from *our* esteem of self.

A disagreement, or conflict, is not necessarily contention or contempt. Contention develops when one or both disagreeing parties are not able to regard the other with love and respect even though there is a disagreement. When one is unable to resolve problems calmly and rationally with another in a spirit of kindness and respect, he is being governed by pride and self-will, not by a godly spirit of love. Whenever disagreements become personal attacks rather than efforts to resolve an issue, it involves pride and is ungodly. Those who believe their views make them more lovable, righteous, or superior than others will exhibit a spirit of anger or intolerance when they are corrected or when offenses and differences in opinions arise. When we are prideful, we cannot disagree with others in matters of emotional significance without feelings of tension, hostility, or disrespect. Disagreements are a normal part of life. It is anger and intolerance towards those who disagree that is not "normal" in the godly sense, and is a manifestation of pride. This is why people who try to control their anger without dealing thoroughly and Biblically with the greater issues involving their pride, fear, jealousy, etc. cannot *ever* conquer their anger. To learn to restrain their angry outbursts if sufficiently motivated (fear of being fired, rejected, or arrested for assault and battery) is sometimes possible, but they NEVER conquer the inward feelings of tension, or restlessness, and always end up redirecting the anger in yet another destructive way, often with great physical manifestations which stem from the chemical changes that the body automatically triggers whenever anger arises internally.

Anger Destroys the Atmosphere of a Home

Proverbs 21:19—It is better to dwell in the wilderness, than with a contentious and an angry woman.

Proverbs 15:17—Better is a dinner of herbs where love is, than a stalled ox and hatred therewith.

Anger destroys the atmosphere that God intended the home to provide. It is rooted in hostility toward others, in a lack of love, and in an unwillingness to overlook or forgive sin. Until a man or woman faces and deals Biblically with his or her own sin of anger, none of the problems in a marriage or home will be resolved. Peace, love, and family intimacy cannot co-exist with anger. A loving family so poor that all they can afford to eat for dinner is Campbell's soup is far better off than an angry family so rich they can afford to eat filet mignon steak every night.

Angry People Influence Others to be Angry

Proverbs 22:24—Make no friendship with an angry man; and with a furious man thou shalt not go: lest thou learn his ways, and get a snare to thy soul.

Ephesians 6:4—And, ye fathers, provoke not your children to wrath: but bring them up in the nurture and admonition of the Lord.

Anger is contagious. It is as much a learned habit as it is a natural human response. The more we expose ourselves or our children to people characterized by anger, the more we will be influenced to react in similar ways. Men who abuse their wives and women who abuse their husbands typically learned their demanding and cruel ways in childhood—from parents, friends, or family. Because anger comes so naturally to sinful and self-centered humans, it is easily learned and incited by exposure to it. Thankfully, because anger is a learned habit, it can be unlearned.

Overcome Anger with Love and Forgiveness

Proverbs 15:1—A soft answer turneth away wrath: but grievous words stir up anger.

Psalm 37:8—Cease from anger, and forsake wrath: fret not thyself in any wise to do evil.

Colossians 3:8-10,12-15—But now ye also put off all these; anger, wrath, malice, blasphemy, filthy communication out of your mouth…Put on therefore, as the elect of God, holy and beloved, bowels of mercies, kindness, humbleness of mind, meekness, longsuffering, forbearing one another, and forgiving one another, if any man have a quarrel against any: even as Christ forgave you, so also do ye. And above all things put on charity [love], which is the bond of perfectness.

Anger is a powerful energy that can be extremely destructive both internally (physically) and externally if it is not directed toward solving problems in righteous ways. God promises believers that He will never allow them to go through a trial without also providing a way of escape and His own supernatural power to meet problems head on through His own grace and strength (*1 Corinthians 10:13*). He assures us that problems of every sort are common to all people, Christians included. Yet only the Christian has God's promise that He is ever present to provide strength, faith, and specific ways to respond. Only a believer can have the assurance that God will always ultimately turn every problem around for good.

When problems arise, as problems will, God wants us to face them and seek His direction and power to resolve the problem His way rather than our own. When we ignore the problem God has allowed, run from the problem, circumvent the problem, blow up at the problem, or hide from the problem, we become prone to sinful expressions of anger, bitterness, and despair. Instead, God instructs us to find the godly means of escape that He has provided to us, so that we might deal with or resolve any problem that comes into our lives. Conquering problems God's way requires us to put off our own ways of dealing with life's difficulties and put on God's ways. Anger is man's way of dealing with problems. Love and forgiveness is God's way.

The following self-evaluation helps you identify areas in your life that may be plagued by anger. In the following chapter we will study Biblical ways you can correct yourself by God's strength and help.

Self-Evaluation

Rate yourself on a one to ten scale in the following areas. Pay particular attention to those areas where you are weakest.

1. How well do I take time to think about what is troubling me before I respond to the trouble?
   0____1____2____3____4____5____6____7____8____9____10

2. How well do I follow the principle of using my energy to attack the problem and not the person?
   0____1____2____3____4____5____6____7____8____9____10

3. How well do I understand and practice God's mercy?
   0____1____2____3____4____5____6____7____8____9____10

4. How well do I refrain from imposing my own goals and demands on others?
   0____1____2____3____4____5____6____7____8____9____10

5. How well am I able to commit all offenses against me into God's hands and refrain from mulling over them or retaliating in any way?
   0____1____2____3____4____5____6____7____8____9____10

6. How well do I really listen to people with genuine concern without thinking ahead?
   0____1____2____3____4____5____6____7____8____9____10

7. How easily do I admit wrong in regard to anger, asking both God and those I hurt to forgive me?
   0____1____2____3____4____5____6____7____8____9____10

8. How well do I find good outlets for my energy and emotional needs?
   0____1____2____3____4____5____6____7____8____9____10

9. How well do I accept failure and imperfection in my life?
   0____1____2____3____4____5____6____7____8____9____10

10. How much effort am I putting into deliberately replacing my sinful acts of anger with godly acts of love?
    0____1____2____3____4____5____6____7____8____9____10

Lesson 11

The Joy of Conquering Anger

A stone is heavy, and the sand weighty; but a fool's wrath is heavier than them both.
Proverbs 27:3

Be not hasty in the spirit to be angry; for anger resteth in the bosom of fools.
Ecclesiastes 7:9

Key Thoughts

LAUGHTER AND JOY
Results from a life filled with godly love and forgiveness

CHAOS AND MISERY
Results from a life lacking godly love and tolerance

Research Question: According to *Matthew 5:22*, what is "the judgment"?

1. A woman with good judgment or _____ is able to control angry reactions by immediately passing over (forgiving/overlooking) the sins and failures of others. *Proverbs 19:11*

2. The woman who learns to resist temptation to quickly react with anger has acquired godly _____ _____. *Proverbs 14:29*

3. Those who respond to the foolish anger of others with quietly spoken words of kindness turn away _____ _____. *Proverbs 15:1*

4. The family of God is to be characterized by righteousness, peace and joy; therefore, Christians should strive to _____ one another. *Romans 14:17-19*

Be not angry that you cannot make others as you wish them to be, since you cannot make yourself as you wish to be. —Thomas A. Kempis

Outward expressions of sinful anger are a lot like fruit growing on a healthy tree that is firmly anchored in the ground by a thriving root system. Plucking fruit off the tree will not stop the production of fruit. It will only temporarily free the tree of its burden. If we want to stop the tree from producing fruit, we'll need to kill its roots—that which feeds the tree and causes fruit to bud and grow in the first place. Anger cannot be destroyed or conquered by plucking it from the tree, or by "managing" it. In order to truly abolish the production of anger, the roots that feed it must be found and destroyed.

"Plucking fruit" might be compared to the world's method of dealing with the destructive nature of anger. Many people readily admit they have no real hope of conquering anger and are quite happy just to have some measure of control over their outbursts. Anger management classes have become a staple strategy in dealing with violence in our society. The reason most people are content to manage anger is because most people don't believe it *can* be conquered. Even Christians sometimes resort to relying on the world's means of anger management, not understanding God has a "program" of anger *abolishment* that goes beyond management. Many Christians fail to realize that unlike the world, they have been given powerful resources that enable them to win the battles against our sinful human nature (flesh). Why would anyone use buckets of water to fight a fire when a fire hydrant and hose was readily available for such an emergency? Why would anyone fight the deadly fire of anger with a "program" when God has provided a far better means than this?

Getting to the "roots" of anger requires a Christian to examine and discover what motivates and feeds anger in the first place. This will be the focus of this chapter. In lesson ten we discussed anger in general terms, identifying the general overall source of anger as man's sinful insistence on having his own way (*Isaiah 53:6*). Anger originates in man's heart, not in external circumstances or other people. We know that preceding angry actions or thoughts are wrong beliefs and desires that do not conform to God's written truth. Truth as God defines truth always sets us free from whatever enslaves and controls us. Killing the roots of anger requires us to discover specific beliefs or desires that feed anger (whether or not that anger is expressed outwardly) and replace the anger with God's truth.

Following are several ways people express anger other than simply blowing up or speaking hatefully.

<u>Ventilation</u>: Blowing up, screaming, yelling, name calling, hitting, slapping, kicking

<u>Displacement</u>: Taking it out on someone else, blaming or accusing others, abusing one's authority over another, putting unreasonable demands on others

<u>Internalize</u>: Privately sulking, pitying self, ruminating on wrongs of others, withdrawal from people or normal activity, tearing apart self, destroying self (as with drugs or alcohol)

<u>Denial</u>: Denying a problem with anger or resentment exists, avoiding dealing with problems, imagining problems are too big or too complicated to solve

<u>Disguised</u>: Sarcasm, biting humor, excessive teasing, inconsiderate actions, crying, and forgetfulness

<u>Physical Manifestations</u>: Panic attacks, anxiety, high blood pressure, headaches, fatigue, gastrointestinal disorders (to name just a few)

There are several common underlying problems that feed sinful anger. These include pride, unforgiveness, hatred, bitterness, unbelief, fear, guilt, jealousy, poor listening habits or communication skills, poor problem resolution skills, inactivity, and a lack of understanding or knowledge (particularly with regard to God's character and faithfulness, His mercy, sovereignty, love, and His work in our lives).

Pride

Pride is the common denominator in *all* sinful anger. No one is able to overcome anger without first thoroughly understanding and dealing with this sin. Pride is an inherent part of our sinful human nature that moves our hearts to react in anger and rebellion when people or circumstances disappoint us, hurt us, or interferes with our desires. Pride fuels our anger and keeps us from graciously accepting the natural consequences of our own sin or the daily imperfections of life. Pride keeps us from responding to mistreatment as Jesus did, and pride blinds us to its danger and causes us to tenaciously deny we could be in need of correction. We are most prone to anger when we refuse to acknowledge the presence and deceptive nature of our pride. This deception is the fertile soil in which pride grows ever more strong.

Pride causes us to depend on our own reasoning, our own strength, and our own efforts to obtain joys and blessings that can only come as we obey and depend on God's timing and will. It blinds us to the dangers of self-reliance and self-will, and generates an attitude of false confidence and determination to live our life in pursuit of what we believe will make us happy. When we are denied, we react in anger, because we have rejected God's wisdom and have chosen instead to lean on our own understanding. The Holy Spirit tells us in *Proverbs 28* that the fool trusts his own heart. The wise, in contrast, start with the premise that we are not wise in and of ourselves and should not rely on our own understanding. "Be not wise in thy own eyes…" A self-sufficient rather than God-sufficient attitude always leads to intolerance of others.

Pride animates us to respond in anger and retaliation when we are hurt or mistreated in any way. Except we are conformed to the image of Christ by God's power and work in our life, we do not react like Jesus. Jesus, as God in human form, understood the sinful nature of those Who persecuted Him and responded without malice toward them. When we are embarrassed, ridiculed, belittled, unjustly criticized, or slandered, our pride prevents us from responding with forgiveness, patience, or gracious words. Instead of ignoring or calmly confronting offenses, we tend to react defensively with outrage when someone treats us unjustly. Instead of rejoicing, as God commands us to do when we are mistreated, we tend to follow our human instincts and defend ourselves. When we suffer at the hands of the unjust, our pride keeps us from committing our case to God and trusting Him to vindicate, judge, or rebuke. Pride keeps us from patiently taking wrong and going on, and pride causes us to worry about the opinions of others, motivating us to protect our reputation with a vengeance if we suspect it is being threatened in any way. Our prideful human bent is to fight for our perceived rights and slander those who slander us—not to love those who hate us or speak well of those who speak evil of us.

Except God give us a humble spirit and fill us with understanding and wisdom, we do not tolerate disappointments or offenses with a calm assurance that God not only sees and hears all, but also uses our disappointments for good in our life and ultimately judges and corrects them righteously and justly. We are more likely to become impatient and use our tongues as weapons to threaten, retaliate, and hurt those who dare to hurt us. In so doing, we become just like them, and miss an opportunity to overcome evil with good by God's power and strength. And is it any wonder? Our pride doesn't allow us to put aside our own feelings for the good of others or the furtherance of God's kingdom. Instead, pride always attempts to overcome evil with evil and imagines such a response is justified.

The righteous counterpart to pride is humility. Those who struggle with anger will find they are powerless to overcome it without confessing the sin of pride and asking God for a humble heart. We need to make a deliberate decision to cultivate humility, beginning with the commitment to study everything the Bible has to say about it. It is helpful to memorize Scriptures in Proverbs that instruct us and warn us of the high cost of pride as well as the rewards of humility. We must be willing to acknowledge the sin of anger to those we hurt and resist the temptation to justify anger or blame it on others or circumstances. The Bible tells us angry people increasingly become more unreasonable, less approachable, and less willing to humble themselves or admit wrong. If you are stubbornly refusing to admit your own sin and cannot see any fault except the faults of others, know that you are blinded with pride and in danger of its terrible consequences. Study *James 4:1-10*.

Read the following passages of Scripture; identify the godly response(s) to suffering,

disappointment, injustice, etc. that is described in each verse. Compare the godly response to a typical ungodly response in one who handles difficulties *his* way rather than *God's*.

Psalm 119:51,61,69,78,85,86,87,95,110,157,161

Matthew 5:11-12

Luke 6:22-23

Luke 6:26-27

Romans 12:12-21

Romans 15:1-3

1 Corinthians 4:12-13

1 Corinthians 6:7

2 Corinthians 4:17-18

Galatians 6:2

Ephesians 4:32

Ephesians 5:2

Philippians 1:29

Philippians 2:4

Colossians 3:13

2 Timothy 2:9-12

James 5:10

1 Peter 2:21-23

1 Peter 3:14-16

1 Peter 4:13-14, 19

2 Thessalonians 1:4

Unforgiveness

A lack of forgiveness toward others shows up in many subtle ways. Those who do not forgive become critical and judgmental toward the flaws and failures they see in others. They are often easily irritated or disgusted by others' sins and demonstrate a low tolerance level for their imperfections. Unforgiveness is commonly manifested as a lack of mercy or patience with people (including children) who do not immediately respond to expectations. People who have difficulty forgiving have

difficulty allowing others to be human, to fail, or to grow. They tend to see only what others are at the moment, not what they can become. They are particularly angry when the failures and sins of others affect their plans or expectations in some way, or when others embarrass or inconvenience them. The focus is on what they want for themselves, not on what is edifying to someone else.

Christians who struggle in the area of forgiveness clearly do not comprehend the magnitude of their own sin debt or God's forgiveness for them. It is as though they believe they deserve God's forgiveness, but others do not—that in some way their own sins are more understandable and forgivable than the sins of others. They are like the servant in *Matthew 18* who was forgiven the equivalent of a billion dollars simply because he asked forgiveness, then refused to forgive a neighbor a few dollars when he too begged for mercy. The worst sins people commit against us are trivial when compared to the sins Christ bore on the cross in our place. A lack of forgiveness is really a lack of understanding with regard to God's love and grace. Having a spirit of unforgiveness blatantly ignores Christ's suffering on our behalf, or His goodness in extending to us His mercy though we did not deserve it.

We are to forgive, not on the basis merit, but on the basis of what God, for Christ's sake, has forgiven us. When we minimize our own sin and magnify the sins of others, we put ourselves in grave spiritual peril. God warns that any refusal to mercifully forgive others from the heart results in torment. He does not tell us exactly what torments He will allow each of us to experience as a result of unforgiveness. However, torment certainly includes depression, anger, anxiety, broken fellowship with Christ, and a barren Christian life. Jesus solemnly reminds us that our Heavenly Father does not forgive or restore fellowship to those who do not forgive others. He will show mercy toward us to the degree we show mercy toward those who fail or sin against us.

Hatred/Lack of Love

The Scriptures are filled with descriptions of genuine godly love. Among them we learn that love is longsuffering, kind, gentle, and not easily provoked. We understand that real love is not merely a description of feeling, attachment, or devotion. *Love* is a word describing deliberate choices of action. Love doesn't take—it gives. Love doesn't tear down—it builds up. Love behaves in specific, predictable ways and is summed up well in *Romans 13:10* where we read that "Love worketh no ill to his neighbor; therefore love is the fulfilling of the law."

When our words and actions hurt or destroy another person, they are not acts of love, but acts of resentment and hatred. Hatred retaliates and hurts those who hurt us, and it will not overlook fault or refrain from gossiping about an enemy. The Bible

tells us "Hatred stirreth up stirifes; but love covereth all sins" (*Proverbs 10:12*). The Scriptures often tie hatred to anger and malicious words. God tells us that a lying tongue *hates* those that are afflicted by it. We are warned that those who hate cause divisions and contention with their lips (*Proverbs 26:24,26*).

The antidote to malicious words and actions is given to believers in *Colossians 3:8-14*. God says, "But now ye also put off all these: anger, wrath, malice, blasphemy, filthy communication out of your mouth. Put on therefore, as the elect of God, holy and beloved, bowels of mercies, kindness, humbleness of mind, meekness, longsuffering; forbearing one another, and forgiving one another, if any man have a quarrel against any: even as Christ forgave you, so also do ye. And above all these things put on charity, which is the bond of perfectness [maturity]."

There are several Christian character qualities that overrule typical human nature, but the one Christian grace that is more powerful than all is charity, or godly love. Attempts to stop hating or resenting are futile unless there is a genuine decision to love as Christ loves. Love is what conquers hate, not the desire to stop hurting or hating. Jesus told us that it is our love for one another that captures the attention of an unbelieving world and identifies us as followers of Him (*John 13:35*). The children of this world angrily hate those they believe hate them. God's children are to demonstrate the difference between good and evil. Just as our Heavenly Father is kind unto the unthankful and to the evil (*Matthew 7:12*), we are to love our enemies, do good to them, and speak well of them.

Bitterness

Bitterness is closely linked to resentment and hatred, developing most often when our reputation is damaged, when pain is inflicted on a loved one, or us, when our expectations are frustrated, and when others do not live up to our desire for them. Bitterness is a subtle germ that wiggles into our life disguised as hurt, disappointment, sorrow, or emotional pain. These emotions seem quite reasonable in times of suffering or when treated unjustly. As a result, they are often cultivated and nurtured until they unexpectedly explode into anger, bitterness, and hatred. Rather than bringing relief or comfort, bitterness strikes as a wild tornado that rips and destroys everything in its path.

Bitterness is produced when we respond to difficult or hurtful events in unbiblical and destructive ways. We might respond by smugly and silently ignoring those we resent. Or, we might respond by attacking them with words designed to hurt or express disagreement or contempt. Sometimes we simply "do nothing" and simmer silently along with those who will commiserate with us. When we enjoy "punishing" those who have hurt us, when we long to see them "put in their place" or destroyed in some way, we are actually putting ourselves in the place of God. God alone has the right to punish and judge sin—and He will. We, however, do not like to commit a hurtful incident to God or trust Him to take care of it in His own time and in His own way. We prefer "helping" God out by inflicting pain and punishment of our own.

Bitterness sees only the pain caused by an offense against a loved one or us—not how God could use the offense for good in our life. Bitterness sees the wrong in others, not the wrong in us. Rather than following the example of Joseph who trusted God to turn around for good that which others intended for evil, the bitter moan as Jacob and say, "All these things are against me!" Study *Genesis 42:36* and *50:19-20*.

Unbelief and Fear

When our hearts are filled with doubts and fears, we become irritable, fretful, and overly sensitive. Fear leads us to believe we must defend and fight for our own protection. When self-preservation consumes our thoughts and actions, our entire life focus becomes our self. This self-preservation is a recipe for anger, particularly when efforts to find security and freedom from fear fail.

The Bible is filled with evidence that God cares for those who believe and trust Him. None who put their trust in Him will be rejected. In *Psalms 9:9-10* we read, "The Lord also will be a refuge for the oppressed, a refuge in times of trouble. And they that know Thy name will put their trust in Thee: for Thou, Lord, hast not forsaken them that seek Thee."

To doubt God's shepherding care for His own children is foolish. This doubt leads to unbelief and fear as well as anger and despair. The Bible tells us, "The foolishness of man perverteth his way: and his heart fretteth against the Lord" (*Proverbs 19:3*). Contrast this passage with *Isaiah 26:3* where God promises, "Thou wilt keep him in perfect peace, whose mind is stayed on Thee: because he trusteth in Thee." What a difference between the one who relies on himself and the one who chooses to put his trust in God.

Israel's unbelief and doubt made them fretful, angry, and defiant. Psalm 78 provides an overview of those who died in the wilderness, fretting against the Lord, refusing to see His love or care for them. Throughout their life they leveled unreasonable charges against God, doubting His mercy, refusing to believe He had their best interest in mind. We see them angry with God, angry with Moses, and angry at one another.

When they tried to take matters into their own hands and protect themselves in their own way, life became more miserable. Unbelief always produces fear, anger, and misery. Ironically, the very thing the unbelieving reject—faith in God's love and trust in God's ways—produces the peace and contentment that calms our spirit and dispels both fear and anger.

Some common fears that fuel anger include fear of God's rejection, fear of God's judgment, fear with regard to one's salvation, fear of loss, fear of death, fear of man, fear of suffering, fear of failure, and fear of loneliness. These are only a few of the many fears that might lead to expressions of frustration and sinful anger. *The God of hope fill you with all joy and peace in believing, that ye may abound in hope through the power of the Holy Ghost (Romans 15:13).*

Guilt

God designed guilt as an alarm system that would provoke man to recognize his sin and come to Him for forgiveness, grace, and mercy. The purpose of guilt is to drive us to the throne of God so we can experience restoration of fellowship and find in Him the strength and help we so desperately need. It confronts us with our need for repentance and points us to the only One Who is able to meet our need and satisfy our longing for relief.

When we begin to comprehend God's love and delight in bringing us to Himself and covering us with His own righteousness, our soul finds rest and encouragement. The marvelous love and forgiveness of God becomes our focus, not our sin. It's as if a great light comes on in our minds and fills us with such love and appreciation for God that we want to sing and find others to love as a result.

The realization of God's love and forgiveness puts life into a different perspective and produces confidence and joy. To the degree the freedom of guilt produces light and joy, the burden of guilt and bondage to sin produces darkness and misery. A guilt-ridden person is not a very loving or happy person. Man is not designed to carry the burden of sin or the weight of guilt. Try as he might to live without a right relationship to God, a person cannot live with guilt without perilous consequence.

Those who refuse to repent of sin and flee to Jesus for forgiveness reject the only means God has provided as a solution to guilt. Such people resort to various human methods of managing guilt in order to escape its grip on their life. They blame others, they minimize the sin, they attempt to drown it out with drugs or alcohol, they engage in non-stop activity to avoid facing it, they adopt religious exercises to make themselves feel righteous, or they engage in humanitarian acts to assure themselves they are good people. Some become self-destructive and abandon themselves to a life of sin and indulgence, while others simply withdraw from life altogether.

When guilt is left unresolved, it brings torment that results in anger, defensiveness, defiance, and selfish pursuit. Lashing out at others, having a "short fuse," irritability and intolerance are just a few of guilt's consequences. Sin must be dealt with on God's terms before anger can be successfully conquered.

There are other reasons a person might experience the effects of guilt other than sin against God. Guilt's effects are torturous to those with an overly sensitive conscience, who tend to blame themselves for the sins and failures of others or accept blame for violating the judgments of man, not God. People who have been excessively abused by others sometimes accept their abuser's accusations out of fear and intimidation. Others learn to accept blame in an effort to please another person or win approval. Still others become so introspective and morbid in their thinking that they imagine they are the cause of whatever goes wrong around them. Accepting blame does not bring relief from false guilt. Guilt can only be resolved by recognizing it as a false accusation against one's self that has no Biblical basis, and rejected.

Finally, guilt is a tormenting slave master to those who lack sufficient faith to confidently believe and accept God's forgiveness when they come to Him for it. Fear and doubt make people circumvent the joy of forgiveness or the realization that our joy is in God's righteousness, not our own. They want to "feel" righteous and acceptable to God in an effort to assure themselves they are forgiven. Instead of looking to the God's Word and relying upon His truths for assurance, they look inside themselves for evidence that they are righteous. This is a dangerous dead end that produces constant anger and unhappiness.

People who fail to understand God's grace and imputed righteousness often strive to achieve (by their own efforts, determination, and will power) the highest degree of goodness or holiness they possibly can. Such behavior is a form of perfectionism that leads to an obsessive drive to excel to such a degree that one does not experience the pain of human failure, weakness, or sin. Perfectionism is a subtle effort to *feel* one's self to be righteous on the basis of one's own self-denial, discipline, or moral excellence. It may also be a means of managing guilt for real, unconfessed sin as a substitute for repentance.

Perfectionists tend to set standards for themselves and others that God Himself does not demand. When they or others do not live up to the rigid expectations they develop, perfectionists typically become angry, irritable, and agitated. Their fear is that failure makes them unacceptable to God; whereas, exact observances of God's law make them acceptable and elicit His divine favor. This error in their understanding makes admitting fault or weakness extremely painful. Not only do they avoid admitting failure, they turn their focus on finding fault in others in an effort to bolster their own sagging ego.

Because perfection can never be attained by human effort, the perfectionist develops a short fuse and tends to be constantly irritated with both himself and others. A perfectionist has a hard time just humbly and thankfully being whatever God allows him to be, accepting failures, limitation, and growth as part of his humanity. He fails to understand God's sanctifying work in his life and his responsibility simply to walk with God and grow in grace. As a result, he fails to see God's progressive work in the lives of other believers as well, and tends to focus on what others appear to be outwardly—not on what God is doing to correct and draw them to Himself or how God is slowly conforming them to His own image.

Jealousy

Few Christians have humility enough to admit, like David, "I was envious at the foolish, when I saw the prosperity of the wicked" (*Psalms 73:3*). More often we describe envy as being hurt or being upset at some injustice. Typically, we compare ourselves to someone we dislike who is prospering or being honored in ways we don't believe they deserve. Though this jealousy is disguised, the implication is that we believe we deserve what someone else is being given more than he or she deserves the honor. Envy is likely if we have been unfairly treated, passed up for a promotion, or deprived recognition for legitimate achievement. Envy, or jealousy, is an expression of discontent over God's provisions and distrust in what God has allowed. Apart from an eternal perspective and trust in God's good and sovereign work in our lives, our human hearts are prone to the evils of envy.

Feelings of resentment and anger springing from jealousy are usually interpreted as legitimate irritations, not as being sinful or destructive. Nothing could be further from the truth. *Proverbs 14:30* teaches that "a sound heart is the life of the flesh; but envy the rottenness of the bones." Envy destroys from the inside out. It eats at one's heart until it poisons a person's thoughts and enslaves his very personality. Envy robs its victim of sleep, of peace, and of joy. Seething below the surface for a time, envy will suddenly erupt in malicious words and cruelty. Envy is destructive, not only because it leads to greater sins and a loss of joy, but also because it is so often excused, denied, and covered up, even when it surfaces in vengeance and wrecks havoc in a life.

The Bible identifies envy as being the direct cause of much anger and cruelty. In fact, the Bible uses the word *cruel* in connection with envy numerous times. "Wrath is cruel, and anger is outrageous; but who is able to stand before envy?" (*Proverbs 27:4*). "Jealousy is cruel as the grave: the coals thereof are coals of fire, which hath a most vehement flame" (*Song of Solomon 8:6*). The various types of cruelties associated with envy and anger are endless. Envy is so treacherous that the Bible makes note of the fact that one cannot resolve it apart from repentance and submission to God.

Anger and destruction are the inseparable companions of envy. Cain murdered Abel because he was jealous of Abel's relationship with God (*Genesis 4:4-8*). Rachel was jealous of Leah (*Genesis 30:1*) and Leah of Rachel (*Genesis 30:15*) causing family turmoil right up to Rachel's death. Laban's sons were jealous of the prosperity of Jacob (*Genesis 31:1*) and enraged their father against him. Joseph's brothers envied the attention their father gave their younger brother (*Genesis 37:4-11*) until they could not speak peaceably at all to Joseph and ultimately sold him into slavery. Even those of godly reputation mar their life and ministry with the sin of jealousy. Miriam and Aaron were envious of Moses' leadership and God-given authority (*Numbers 12:1-10*). Saul was so envious of David that it consumed his life until he vowed to kill David (*1 Samuel 20:31*). The Bible tells us that the priests who plotted the crucifixion of Jesus did so because they were jealous of Him (*Matthew 27:18; John 11:47*).

Lack of Physical and Mental Activity

God has made each of us in such a way that we all possess the potential to do everything He has designed us to do. Our minds need to be challenged appropriately with good and constructive things. Our bodies need balanced food and activity that will stimulate strength and proper function. To maintain spiritual, physical, and emotional well-being, we must have times of rest, diversion, and outlets to expend mental and physical energy in good ways. God intends for us to choose constructive outlets for energy and service in building God's kingdom. Usefulness in the body of Christ (local church) prevents loneliness as well as the sadness that results when we wrongly judge ourselves or become self-focused. Using and developing spiritual gifts and talents that are given by God provides a wonderful sense of joy in God's love and acceptance. These things all serve as important "inoculations" against depression and anger. Never underestimate the big results that can come from small changes in these areas!

Poor Listening and Communication Skills

Angry people tend to talk more than listen. This leads to surmising, drawing hasty (and often incorrect) conclusions, and reacting impulsively. Angry people are quick to judge and slow to listen before they react. Even when they are not talking, they may *not* be listening intently in an effort to weigh information carefully or understand what another person is saying. Their impatience and self-interest make them prone to tuning out in boredom or *thinking ahead* of the person they are listening to in order to

NOTES

begin constructing their own story or defense. They imagine, in error, that keeping themselves quiet when another is talking is the same as listening. It is not!

Angry people tend to be opinionated people who have developed the habit of dogmatically drawing their own conclusions based on their own perceptions and hanging on to them tenaciously—even when evidence is clearly stacked against them. They tend to surmise instantly without careful investigation of facts, and then repeat their conclusions as if they were fact. Reasoning with an angry person is next to impossible because they lack sufficient self-discipline or self-denial to work at listening patiently and communicating effectively. They are often determined to prove their own way or establish their own superiority or authority over others rather than humbly listening.

People struggling with anger dramatically improve their ability to control sinful reactions when they work at increasing their patience, love, and respect for others' opinions and feelings and learn better communication and listening skills. Simply disciplining one's self to suspend judgment and take the time to understand before one draws a conclusion resolves much anger.

Poor Problem Resolution Skills

People characterized by anger often develop the habit of attacking *people* in supposed self-defense rather than attacking the *problem*. This sometimes includes attacking and berating himself or herself, or attacking people covertly rather than openly. This sinful practice is the result of failing to confront and work out problems Biblically with the means God has provided for us. Working out problems in a godly way requires us to be humble, to be focused on the issue and not ourselves, to be in control of our own spirit, to be ready to love and forgive. These disciplines do not come naturally to any of us. They must be learned and practiced *deliberately*.

God tells us that the Christian is so protected by God that he is *never* allowed to experience a problem without also be given sufficient strength and God-given grace to deal with the problem righteously. Furthermore, the Christian is reminded that His Heavenly Father is faithful—He *cannot* lie and *never* fails to do exactly as He has promised. God Himself assures us that He *always* provides a way to escape when the trials of life assault us. Finally, we are told that while we suffer the same difficulties and trials in this world as those who do not know God, we do not suffer anything without a purpose and we are always delivered from every affliction in some God-given way (*1 Corinthians 10:13*).

NOTES

Before we can learn to deal with problems in a way that pleases God and elicits His blessing, we must understand and believe all of these important truths. We read in *1 Corinthians 10:13*, "There hath no temptation [trial] taken you but such as is common to man; but God is faithful, who will not suffer [allow] you to be tempted [tried] above that ye are able; but will with the temptation also make a way to escape, that ye may be able to bear it." Again the Holy Spirit tells us through David that "The righteous [saved] cry, and the Lord heareth and delivereth them out of all their troubles…Many are the afflictions of the righteous; but the Lord delivereth him out of them all" (*Psalms 34:17,19*). Notice the words God uses to express the emphatic certainty of the truth—*no, will not, will, and all*.

When we are faced with any kind of trial, or problem, our human tendency is to either blow up in anger because we don't like what is happening, run the opposite direction because we don't want to deal with it, clam up out of fear and despair, or attempt to circumvent it in an effort to find an easier way to deal with it. None of these methods are righteous and none can be employed without painful consequences. God's way is to acknowledge and confront the problem, seek God's Word for direction in finding the way of escape God has provided, obey the Scriptural admonition for dealing with the particular problem, and then wait and trust God to intervene to do what we are powerless to do.

Those who desire to face and confront problems by God's strength, in God's way, will first want to seek God's wisdom on God's terms. Study Proverbs chapter 2 and James chapter 1. When we acknowledge that our ways fail and our human reasoning is insufficient to recognize and resolve problems righteously, when we seek humility and wisdom first, when we are certain that we are willing to submit our will to God and allow Him to use the problem for our good and future joy, and when we ask God to help us properly discern the problem or provocation (taking the necessary time to identify the source of anger)…then, and only then, are we facing the problems Biblically and taking the proper steps toward a solution.

The following exercise will assist in helping you learn to recognize and intercept starting points of anger. Each time you become aware you are angry (or beginning to sense the rising tension that precedes anger), answer the following five questions in a notebook. Note the particular recurring situation that you react to in anger.

1. What am I angry about?

2. Is there something I can change to make the situation more tolerable or solve the problem?

3. Is there something I can change about me?

NOTES

4. What Biblical instructions do I know I have failed to obey regarding this situation?

5. Would Jesus be angry over this?

Following are some things to remember that will encourage you to learn godly ways of handling anger.

Cease justifying anger. Quickly recognize and admit anger and practice principles of repentance. Follow repentance with restitution to those who you have offended and with thanksgiving for God's love, mercy, and forgiveness. Learn to obey God's rules concerning anger and look for righteous solutions to problems and trials. Attack the problem, not the person, and not yourself. Cease demanding perfection in others. Recognize God's sovereignty. God will deal with both the wicked who oppress His children and other Christians who oppress His children. He will do this in His own way, in His own time. Do all you can to work out problems with others in a Biblical way with a Biblical attitude, and then entrust your case to Him. Rest in the knowledge that He is faithful to deal with others. God alone can accurately judge hearts and administer correction.

Replace acts of anger. Put off bitterness, abusive words, wrath, and self-centeredness. Replace them by putting on acts of love such as patience, kindness, humility, and forgiveness. This is one of the most important keys to overcoming anger. We can only conquer habitual anger, unkindness, or unkind words, etc. by developing new habits of deliberate acts of kindness, love, and forgiveness. New godly reactions and habits must replace the old, sinful ones. Therefore, the primary focus must be on developing godly actions rather than pouring effort into merely trying to control ungodly reactions.

Remember that a failure to work out problems Biblically or to discuss them eventually produces tension and discouragement. This leads to various expressions of anger. Ignoring problems God has commanded us to deal with in a particular way leads to unhappiness and irritability because we are not living obediently toward God, and thus cannot receive the peace of the Holy Spirit.

In Conclusion:

Anger *cannot* be conquered without dealing with its underlying spiritual motivations and causes. Though they may not appear to have anything to do with anger on the surface, these motivations *are* the roots that feed our anger and keep it from being overcome. By studying the roots of anger and learning to replace them with the roots of righteous contentment, joy, and peace, you will discover in time that God has accomplished in your heart what no one and nothing else could accomplish before. We are better able to understand and conquer our human tendency toward anger when we develop a thorough understanding of the attributes of God with particular emphasis on God's character—His faithfulness, His mercy, His sovereignty, His love, and His work in our lives.

Lesson 12

The Joy of Happy Thoughts

In the multitude of my thoughts within me, Thy comforts delight my soul.
Psalm 94:19

Finally, brethren, whatsoever things are true, whatsoever things are honest, whatsoever things are just, whatsoever things are pure, whatsoever things are lovely, whatsoever things are of good report; if there be any virtue, and if there be any praise, think on these things.
Philippians 4:8

Key Thoughts

A Pure and Happy Heart
A mind occupied with good and accurate thoughts

A Tormented and Restless Heart
A mind occupied with self-centered, sinful, or inaccurate thoughts

---

Research Question: *Proverbs 16:3* states that "Thy thoughts shall be established." What do you think this means? Note: The word *heart* in the Bible is often referring to our thoughts and things we have accepted and stored in our memory as truth. The word includes the emotions that arise out of our mental evaluations and thoughts. Our heart, in the Bible sense, represents all that we are inside, including our sin nature. Whatever occupies our thoughts determines what we are and will become.

1. The woman who dwells on happy things has a _____ _____, but the woman who dwells on sorrowful things becomes depressed. *Proverbs 15:13*

2. There is a relationship between how a woman _____ and how a woman feels physically. *Proverbs 15:13*

3. Thinking about God's _____ causes us to praise Him and be happy. *Psalm 48:9-14*

4. A woman is delighted and comforted when she _____ _____ _____. *Psalm 94:19*

5. Before a woman experiences the peace of God which passeth understanding, she must rejoice, be thankful, pray for her requests, and _____ _____ _____ _____. *Philippians 4:4-8*

Most people are about as happy as they make up their minds to be. —Abraham Lincoln

What We Think About Is What We Are

How we think, what we think, and what we store in our memory have a tremendous capacity to determine our disposition, our behavior, and our attitudes. What we choose to believe and dwell on is of utmost importance, for it becomes a part of all that we are. We eventually act consistent with what we think and what we believe. The more we think about something, the more it becomes a part of our memory and personality. We think, then we speak, then we act, and then we become. Yet our thoughts don't stop at what we become, for what we become has consequences, good and bad, and eventually determines our innermost joy or sorrow. In essence, our thought life determines our destiny.

We cannot change what we are or how we feel emotionally, without changing what and how we think. Actions always originate in our thought life.

Even the things we are no longer consciously aware of but have stored in our memory, affect our conscious decisions, behavior patterns, and instant reactions. This is why the Bible warns, "Keep thy heart (thoughts) with all diligence, for out of it are the issues of life" (*Proverbs 4:23*).

Words that are spoken when our guard is down betray the private thoughts of our heart and reveal its condition. Jesus reminds us that "out of the abundance of the heart the mouth speaketh" (*Matthew 12:34b*).

We sometimes deceive ourselves into believing we can think whatever we want and keep those thoughts separate from how we act. For example, many people indulge in imaginary fantasies of immoral activities believing they are "non-sexual" and harmless. Because thoughts are engaged in secret, we assume they are not damaging or sinful. Others ruminate repeatedly on hateful thoughts of others, believing their thoughts are justified, not sinful or destructive. The Bible tells us differently. *Proverbs 24:9* says, "The thought of foolishness is sin…" and in *Psalms 44:21*, "Shall not God search this out? For He knoweth the secrets of the heart." God warns, "Thou shalt not hate thy brother in thine heart…" (*Leviticus 19:17*).

Not only does God see and know our thoughts, He judges the secret sins committed in the hidden corners of our minds as well. "For God shall bring every work into judgment, with every secret thing, whether it be good, or whether it be evil" (*Ecclesiastes 12:14*). David understood the dangers of sins committed in secret. He prayed, Lord cleanse me from "secret faults" (*Psalm 19:12*). We are warned that we can only hide sinful thoughts for so long before they become openly manifest in our life (*Proverbs*

NOTES

26:23-28; note verse *26*). Thoughts are seeds sown in secret that grow into full grown plants of sin or righteousness.

People gravitate toward whatever they think about most. Even people who do not believe the Bible recognize that people become whatever they think about—either good or bad. They also recognize the fact that happy people are people who think differently than unhappy people.

The world uses its knowledge and observations of this basic human behavior to market every kind of self-improvement, success motivation program imaginable. They often seize what is actually a very simple and profound Biblical truth, complicate the truth so it sounds deep and professional (and therefore more credible) and then sell it to unsuspecting consumers at unbelievable prices. Christian, you do not need to pay hundreds of dollars for a success seminar; just read your Bible and practice it!

God says, "For as [a man] thinketh in his heart, so is he" (*Proverbs 23:7a*). In many ways our mind is like a computer. We only get out of it what we program into it. If we feed our minds soap operas and romance novels, we will eventually think and act like the characters we spend so much time observing. If we constantly tell ourselves we are a failure and can't do anything right, we are programming ourselves to fail. If we think about all the things we don't like about people, or how they have mistreated us, we become critical and hateful.

Thankfully, becoming what we think about works just as well in reverse. If we tell ourselves on a daily basis "I can do all things through Christ which strengtheneth me" (*Philippians 4:13*), we discover we really can do all God wants us to do. If we feed our minds on Scripture we discover, as David did, how meditating on the powerful Word of God gives victory over sin (*Psalm 119:11*). If we bring every thought into captivity to the obedience of Christ as we have been instructed to do in *2 Corinthians 10:4-5*, we discover happy freedom from the bondage and misery wrong thinking always produces. Truth sets us free from all that would rob us of our joy and all that would keep us in bondage to sin; therefore, God commands us to choose deliberately to think on what is true. Study *John 8:31-36* and *Philippians 4:8*.

Our Faces Give Away Our Thoughts

If you could listen in on the private thoughts of a sullen or irritated person, you would discover how unhappy his thoughts are. On the other hand, if you could interrupt the thoughts of an obviously joyful and content person who doesn't know his thoughts are being observed, you would discover his thoughts to be very pleasant and uplifting. Our countenance is merely the outward reflection of what we are inwardly thinking. The Bible says, "A merry heart maketh a cheerful countenance: but by sorrow of the heart the spirit is broken" (*Proverbs 15:13*).

Pleasant, happy people are pleasant and happy because they *think* about pleasant and happy things. They follow God's thought prescription in Philippians 4:8, whether they do so intentionally or not. Happy people do not spend time thinking morbid *what if* thoughts about some terrible calamity that might happen. They do not entertain critical thoughts or imagine worst-case scenarios or speculate about evil possibilities. They do not dwell on thoughts that are depressing, anxious, fearful, angry, self-centered, jealous, or impatient. Therefore, they do not reflect depression, anxiety, anger, pride, jealousy, or impatience on their faces or in their attitudes.

No matter how hard we may try to hide it, sinful, negative thoughts show up in subtle little ways on our face and in our mannerisms. We might not think we are giving ourselves away and we may be secretly convinced that we are doing a great job hiding how we feel. Yet others do detect the subtle clues that are always there and typically react to those clues even when they do not acknowledge what they sense intuitively by our subtle behavior.

The right way to deal with your attitude, words, and countenance is not to paste on a pretend smile, but to deal with the thoughts of your heart. Change the way you think, and your countenance will automatically change with no other effort. Cover your sinful thought patterns with a phony smile, and you will quickly become emotionally exhausted whenever you need to be around people. In fact, you may not enjoy being with people much at all, or at least, not for extended periods of time.

Acting happy and loving require an enormous amount of effort when the inward thoughts of the heart are predominantly unhappy and unloving.

The way one thinks is a learned behavior that becomes a habit. Thankfully, because our thought life is learned, it can be unlearned; it is merely a matter of learning new and godly habits of thinking and practicing over and over until it is second nature. Try spending some time recalling things you do well and things you are looking forward to. If you are using this Bible study as a group, break up in pairs and tell your partner what you admire or appreciate about them most. Notice the difference in the way you feel after you have thought on these pleasant and edifying things rather than on things such as what you dread or what you believe you do *not* do well.

List 5 things you do well.

1.

2.

3.

4.

5.

List 3 things you are looking forward to.

1.

2.

3.

How Our Thoughts Can Bring Comfort and Joy

Most people deceive themselves into believing they are comforting themselves or *getting on top of things* by thinking about their problems, their wants, or their upsetting circumstances. Sometimes even prayer is used as a means to dwell excessively but "legitimately" on our own problems or on ourselves. Focusing on our problems never resolves them or brings peace to our hearts. Instead, this inward focus breeds selfishness, self-centeredness, depression, and great discontent.

Thinking unbiblically is counterproductive in every way. Rather than producing joy, it produces unrelenting fear and sorrow. Before long we become so full of self-pity that we become a "walking bruise." If anyone so much as *bumps* us with a correction or discomfort, we protest and scream in pain. Self-focused people are always unhappy, over-sensitive people.

The Bible says, "Great peace have they which love Thy law and nothing shall offend them" (*Psalm 119:165*). People who apply the Scriptures to their lives are not focused on themselves at all. They are focused on living for the Lord, building His kingdom, and growing in their knowledge of the Lord Jesus Christ. They see problems as opportunities for spiritual growth, not as reasons to abandon their faith. Consequently, they are not easily offended or spiritually derailed. The Bible says, "Thou wilt keep him in perfect peace whose mind is stayed on Thee" (*Isaiah*

26:3a). The person whose mind is focused on Christ and pleasing Him is at peace. In contrast, the person whose mind is focused on himself is in great turmoil.

List five good thoughts you can think about instead of thinking about yourself, your problems, or your disappointments.

1.

2.

3.

4.

5.

How Thinking in the Present Affects Our Happiness

We develop a much happier disposition when we learn to focus our minds on the present moment, rather than dwelling on what happened yesterday or what could happen tomorrow. People who rehash past events over and over live in a past they cannot change. They paralyze themselves emotionally and rarely enjoy life or accomplish much.

Those who are constantly fretting about tomorrow fare no better. They live in a future that God has not revealed to them or yet given them grace to handle. They want to deal with what *might* happen, not what God actually allows to happen. There is a reason that Jesus taught us to pray "give us this day our daily bread" and not "give us this month our monthly bread." He said today's problems are sufficient for us to deal with. "Take, therefore, no thought for the morrow: for the morrow shall take thought for the things of itself. Sufficient unto the day is the evil thereof" (*Matthew 6:34*). God wants us to put the past behind us and leave the future to Him. Our concern is to be centered on what God expects us to do *today*.

Prudent planning, preparation, and goal setting are constructive. However, when the planning becomes fretting, speculating, and anxious contemplation, it is worry. Worry is not only sinful; it is exhausting and destructive.

Sometimes we worry because we are not able to make our plans and then simply entrust our life to a God we believe is intimately involved in our daily life as our Shepherd and Guide. Other times we worry when we are unwilling to accept life's

ups and downs. The dread of discomfort causes us to think ahead anxiously in an effort to rearrange life on our own terms in order to avoid any possible suffering or disruption to our plans. It is as if we believe we have the ability to overrule what God allows or disallows. Habitually thinking this way keeps people nervous, edgy, and unhappy. This thinking simply doesn't work the way we imagine it will. Pay attention to negative *what-if* thinking. When you catch yourself imagining a worst case scenario, say to yourself "Stop!" Then, change the *what-if* to make the thought true and good. For instance, if you catch yourself thinking, "What if I fail this test?" and imagine how terrible it would be if you did, change your thought to, "What if I do great!" and imagine how good that would be.

Reverse 3 bad what-if statements to make them 3 good ones.

Wrong Thought: What if _____

Change to: What if _____

Wrong Thought: What if _____

Change to: What if _____

Wrong Thought: What if _____

Change to: What if _____

How People Influence Our Thinking and Happiness

People are extremely influenced by whomever and whatever they choose to be around. We automatically pick up gestures, words, and attitudes of people we spend time with because their input is what our minds take in.

People tend to become a part of their immediate environment. Consequently, we influence the people around us, including our impressionable little children, just as the people and things around us influence the way we think and behave. Being with happy, productive people encourages us to be happy and productive. Being with spiritually-minded people encourages us to think more spiritually. Being with negative and critical people encourages us to think more negatively. And being with godless people encourages us to think, act, and consequently become ungodly.

No wonder God places such importance on coming together for church services, spending time in prayer and Bible reading, and choosing wise companions. *"He that walketh with wise men shall be wise; but a companion of fools shall be destroyed"* (*Proverbs 13:20*).

List 3 people you can spend time with who influence you to think right. Why do they influence you in a constructive way?

1.

2.

3.

How Thankfulness Affects Our Thinking and Happiness

Learning the secret of *thinking thankfully* will get you through life's toughest times with a joyful heart. God commands (yes, commands) us to give thanks in the same context that He commands us to petition Him for help and direction. It all goes together. God does not say *feel thankful*. We do not necessarily *feel* thankful when we are having a bad day. God does say to *be* thankful and to *give* thanks—for everything. "In *everything* give thanks, for this is the will of God in Christ Jesus concerning you" (*1 Thessalonians 5:18*). Thankfulness on our part always precedes God's blessings and answered prayer.

Thankfulness in the midst of a trial requires obedience, faith, and enough spiritual maturity to see the potential good that God will cause to come out of adversity rather than the present adversity itself. Thankfulness in times of prosperity and joy requires recognition that God is the Giver of every good gift, the Supplier of every need, and the Creator of all genuine love and joy. He is the tenderhearted Lover of our soul, the selfless Friend who delights to bring joy into our life. Thankfulness to God is an acknowledgement that we believe He is the source of all blessing. It is a token of our love and sincerity; an expression that springs from a grateful heart that recognizes every good thing comes out of God's grace and love, not from anything we do or are apart from God. To give praise or thanksgiving to anyone or anything without giving praise and thanksgiving to God is like thanking the bank for cashing a million dollar check while ignoring the person who gave the million dollars to us as a gift.

The more we learn to be thankful and thank God for everything, even when we don't feel like it, the more we feel thankful. Consequently, we also experience joy

NOTES

and peace. In the Bible, thanksgiving is most often spoken of in the same context of praise, singing, joyfulness, and humble recognition of God's love and care for His people. "Make a joyful noise unto the Lord, all ye lands. Serve the Lord with gladness; come before his presence with singing. Know ye that the Lord He is God; it is He that hath made us, and not we ourselves; we are His people, and the sheep of His pasture. Enter into His gates with thanksgiving, and into His courts with praise; be thankful unto Him, and bless His name. For the Lord is good; His mercy is everlasting; and His truth endureth to all generations" (*Psalm 100*). As long as I am constantly thinking about how good God is, and how thankful I am for all He's given, I cannot possibly entertain depressing, defeating thoughts. The two cannot possibly be thought simultaneously. The spirit of praise and gratefulness lifts the spirit and conquers depression and despair like nothing else can. God blesses the grateful spirit and uses it to give us supernatural peace, joy, and a wonderful sense of security and well being, even in the midst of life's greatest storms. Sustaining any emotion requires thought, regardless if that emotion is good or bad.

Find thankful people, those who can truly give thanks in everything, and you will discover that they are happy people. People who have learned to trust God with the outcome of every distressing event in life also learn how to have a great sense of humor as well. Thankfulness generates hope and optimism. It allows us to see the light side of every circumstance, and in many instances, thankfulness opens the door to laughter.

When we are able to have fun and see the humorous side of our daily life, we feel better, work more productively, and are more enjoyable to other people. Those with a thankful, merry heart have a continual feast, even in the desert times of life (*Proverbs 15:15*).

List 10 things you can be thankful for.

1.
2.
3.
4.
5.

6.
7.
8.
9.
10.

How Our Thinking Helps or Hurts Our Relationships

Our thoughts are a powerful influence in all our relationships, either for good or bad. Far too often, unbridled thoughts are at the root of a destroyed marriage, home, or friendship. One's thought life has the capacity to utterly demolish loving relationships.

God describes genuine love in *1 Corinthians 13*. In that well-known passage there is a little phrase that says, love "thinketh no evil." Love is not self-centered, as so many of our hateful thoughts toward others are. Love does NOT think evil of another! Hateful, evil thoughts *always* produce anger and destroy love. On the other hand, good, loving thoughts have the power to generate love in our hearts for others.

If you think about your spouse or friend's bad qualities and flaws (and everyone has some) long enough, you will soon forget all their many good qualities and their wonderful potential for growth. You will quickly forget that you are no less a mortal sinner than they, and you will tend to forget every Bible exhortation to love your neighbor and overlook faults.

If you keep up a negative, sinful flow of thoughts long enough, you will begin to despise your neighbor in your heart instead of loving him. You will become irritable with him, and find it harder and harder to control your biting words. You will cease enjoying him, and being together will become miserable for you both. All of this comes about, not because of what your spouse or friend is or isn't, but because you chose to dwell on faults and failures rather than loving thoughts for another.

This same destructive process will occur if you think negatively about a church member, a co-worker, a family member, or even your children. This is why God commands us not to hate our brother in our heart (thoughts) or hold any grudge against him (*Leviticus 19:17*). Instead, we are to think loving, kind, and merciful thoughts toward our neighbor—whether our neighbor is our closest family member, a church member, or a co-worker.

Pick two people you are having trouble loving. List 5 good qualities of each. Pray for each person, thanking God for each of the qualities you listed. Next, find opportunities to mention these good qualities to someone else. Spread some "good" gossip and see how God gives joy as a result.

NOTES

Proverbs 15:23—A man hath joy by the answer of his mouth: and a word spoken in due season, how good is it!

Person One
1.
2.
3.
4.
5.

Person Two
1.
2.
3.
4.
5.

Five Deadly Thought Patterns

What we choose to think about, good or bad, is potentially habit forming. The more we think in certain ways, the more we actually gravitate toward repeating and dwelling on our familiar thought patterns. If these thought patterns follow the guidelines given by the Lord, the result will be a peace that passes understanding. If, however, our thoughts are allowed to wander and dwell on things that are ungodly or destructive to us, they will eventually alter our attitude, our perceptions, and our inner happiness.

There are five particularly destructive thought patterns that destroy our peace and joy—guilty thoughts, fearful thoughts, ungrateful thoughts, angry thoughts, and self-centered thoughts. The way to Biblically change our thought patterns is to repent of our sinful thoughts and replace them, not merely try to stop them.

Guilty thoughts must be replaced by thoughts of thankfulness and awe of God's complete forgiveness after we have repented and acknowledged our sin. "I, even I am He that blotteth out thy trangressions for Mine own sake, and will not rememer thy sins. Put Me in remembrane; let us plead together; declare thou, that thou mayest be justified" (*Isaiah 43:25-26*). "Blessed [how happy] is he whose transgression is forgiven, whose sin is covered" (*Psalms 32:1*).

Fearful and anxious thoughts must be replaced by thoughts of God's love and care and absolute control of our lives. "And we have known and believed the love that God hath to us. God is love; and he that dwelleth in love dwelleth in God, and God in him… There is no fear in love; but perfect love casteth out fear: because fear hath torment…" (*1 John 4:16, 18*).

Ungrateful thoughts must be replaced with thoughts of praise and thanksgiving in every situation and for every provision God gives, for we deserve nothing. "It is a good thing to give thanks unto the Lord, and to sing praises unto Thy name, O most High; to show forth Thy lovingkindness in the morning, and Thy faithfulness every night. For thou, Lord, hast made me glad through Thy work; I will triumph in the works of Thy hands" (*Psalms 92:1-4*).

Angry thoughts must be replaced with thoughts of mercy and love for others. "With all lowliness and meekness, with longsuffering, forbearing one another in love; be ye kind one to another, tenderhearted, forgiving one another, even as God for Christ's sake hath forgiven you" (*Ephesians 4:2,32*).

Self-centered thoughts must be replaced with thoughts that focus outwardly on ways we can serve the Lord effectively, and meet the needs of others. "For God is not unrighteous to forget your work and labor of love, which ye have showed toward His name, in that ye have ministered to the saints, and do minister" (*Hebrews 6:10*).

In conclusion, Paul says in *Philippians 4:8*, "Finally, brethren, whatsoever things are true, whatsoever things are honest, whatsoever things are just, whatsoever things are pure, whatsoever things are lovely, whatsoever things are of good report; if there be any virtue, and if there be any praise, think on these things."

Family Fight-Right Ground Rules

1. Fights must be limited to one issue at a time.

2. Absolutely no name-calling or sarcasm allowed. You may attack the issue but never each other.

3. You may not bring up past offenses or failures. Any attempt to do so must be recognized as a sinful unwillingness to forgive.

4. Any expectation that another should *understand* without our telling them must be relinquished.

5. All fights are to take place at the kitchen table, den, or other specified fighting location. All participants must remain seated while fighting.

6. No fighting may take place past 10:00 P.M. (adults) or 8:00 P.M. (children).

7. No inappropriate fighting may take place in the presence of children (if husband and wife are fighting) or uninvolved friends or family (no off-the-top-of-the-head fighting allowed). Destructive fighting should never be allowed.

8. All participants must be allowed *equal time* to express grievances, as well as equal listening time. No one will draw conclusions until all involved have a chance to express themselves.

9. All participants must be willing to negotiate solutions, not just vent or appease anger.

10. The ultimate goal of every person fighting is to be a peacemaker and problem solver in the spirit of love, according to *Colossians 3:13-14*.

Note: All participants must recognize unchecked contention to be the result of pride. Anger is an emotion as much as a reaction. When one senses the instantaneous emotion of anger, he must keep it "in check" and refuse to express it in sinful ways. (See *Ephesians 4*)

Note: All must be willing to ultimately give up their rights if necessary. Any unwillingness to negotiate a solution or tackle secret resentments must be recognized as indifference, which is the greatest enemy of love and harmony in a relationship. (See *Proverbs 13:10*)

Family Fight Right Conclusion

Confrontations conducted with an attitude of humility and love are a necessary and constructive part of learning to get along together and communicate with one another. However, any failure to abide by the ground rules must be acknowledged and forgiven.

Obviously, many of these guidelines won't be appropriate or practical to use with toddlers and very small children. However, if you will gradually incorporate them with your small children and demonstrate them to your children by using them yourself, you'll find the *rules* become an accepted and natural way of handling problems as the years go on.

Establishing family rules and consistent patterns of behavior when your children are still too young to fully understand will ultimately result in older children and teenagers who will handle fighting in a constructive way instead of the traditional *raise the roof* destructive way.

It is important that your children have opportunities to observe a godly, controlled way of disagreeing that resolves conflicts. Ultimately children do whatever they see, whether good or bad. To some extent, it is constructive and profitable for children to see Mom and Dad disagree and resolve conflicts Biblically and lovingly. It is not constructive to openly discuss matters that children are not yet emotionally able to handle or understand. It is also not constructive and profitable for children to observe Mom and Dad behaving in a disrespectful, petty, selfish, or uncontrolled manner. When this occurs, be sure the children also observe Mom and Dad acknowledging their behavior as sinful and seeking one another's forgiveness. Children are greatly blessed when parents display humility in this way, and they will imitate it in their future relationships and marriage.

Remember that your goal is to encourage your children to Biblically solve their disagreements with as little of your intervention as possible. Therefore, it is preferable to try to supervise more than intervene. Learning how to disagree properly will help our children learn how to live, for conflict resolution is a skill that will benefit them in every area of their future life. Take the time to learn and teach it! Your family life will be happier for it!

A p p e n d i x

THINGS THAT GOD SAYS MAKE US HAPPY

This book of the law shall not depart out of thy mouth; but thou shalt meditate therein day and night, that thou mayest observe to do according to all that is written therein: for then thou shalt make thy way prosperous, and then thou shalt have good success.
Joshua 1:8

And these things write we unto you, that your joy may be full.
1 John 1:4

Psalm 1: The Path to a Happy Life

Happy (blessed) is the person who:

1. Doesn't follow the philosophies of the unsaved or seek their guidance.

2. Doesn't associate with rebellious or ungodly people.

3. Doesn't indulge in criticizing others, pointing out other's flaws, or harboring grudges against others.

4. Does diligently study and follow the principles of God's Word, seeking guidance from the Scriptures and learning God's ways.

The result is a productive and, consequently, happy life in which God fulfills three promises:

1. A genuinely fruitful life.

2. Continual fruitfulness that lasts because it is grounded in eternal values and rooted in God's Word.

3. Works that prosper by God's strength and power.

God's Way of Bringing Happiness into a Life

Knowing the Word of God

Psalm 19:8—The statutes of the LORD are right, rejoicing the heart: the commandment of the LORD is pure, enlightening the eyes.

Psalm 119:111—Thy testimonies have I taken as an heritage for ever: for they are the rejoicing of my heart.

Psalm 119:162—I rejoice at Thy word, as one that findeth great spoil.

Psalm 119:165—Great peace have they which love Thy law: and nothing shall offend them.

Jeremiah 15:16—Thy words were found, and I did eat them; and Thy word was unto me the joy and rejoicing of mine heart: for I am called by Thy name, O LORD God of hosts.

Trusting in God

Psalm 28:7—The LORD is my strength and my shield; my heart trusted in Him, and I am helped: therefore my heart greatly rejoiceth; and with my song will I praise Him.

Psalm 63:7—Because thou hast been my help, therefore in the shadow of thy wings will I rejoice.

Proverbs 16:20—He that handleth a matter wisely shall find good: and whoso trusteth in the LORD, happy is he.

Fellowshiping With Other Believers

Psalm 133:1—Behold, how good and how pleasant it is for brethren to dwell together in unity!

Philippians 2:1-2—If there be therefore any consolation in Christ, if any comfort of love, if any fellowship of the Spirit, if any bowels and mercies, fulfill ye my joy, that ye be likeminded, having the same love, being of one accord, of one mind.

Philippians 2:17-18—Yea, and if I be offered upon the sacrifice and service of your faith, I joy, and rejoice with you all. For the same cause also do ye joy, and rejoice with me.

Meditating on God

Psalm 63:5—My soul shall be satisfied as with marrow and fatness; and my mouth shall praise Thee with joyful lips.

Psalm 104:34—My meditation of Him shall be sweet: I will be glad in the LORD.

Singing to the Lord

Psalm 71:23—My lips shall greatly rejoice when I sing unto Thee; and my soul, which thou hast redeemed.

Psalm 100:1-2—Make a joyful noise unto the LORD, all ye lands. Serve the LORD with gladness: come before His presence with singing.

Having a Heart Right With God

Psalm 97:11—Light is sown for the righteous, and gladness for the upright in heart.

Desiring Spiritual Things

Psalm 107:9—For He satisfieth the longing soul, and filleth the hungry soul with goodness.

Winning Souls to Christ

Psalm 126:5-6—They that sow in tears shall reap in joy. He that goeth forth and weepeth, bearing precious seed, shall doubtless come again with rejoicing, bringing his sheaves with him.

Fearing the Lord. Walking in His Ways.

Psalm 128:1—Blessed is every one that feareth the LORD; that walketh in His ways.

Psalm 144:15—Happy is that people, that is in such a case: yea, happy is that people, whose God is the LORD.

Proverbs 29:18—Where there is no vision, the people perish: but he that keepeth the law, happy is he.

Ecclesiastes 2:26—For God giveth to a man that is good in His sight wisdom, and knowledge, and joy: but to the sinner He giveth travail, to gather and to heap up, that he may give to him that is good before God. This also is vanity and vexation of spirit.

Acts 2:28—Thou hast made known to me the ways of life; thou shalt make me full of joy with Thy countenance.

Achieving Through Hard Work

Psalm 128:2—For thou shalt eat the labour of thine hands: happy shalt thou be, and it shall be well with Thee.

Ecclesiastes 2:24—There is nothing better for a man, than that he should eat and drink, and that he should make his soul enjoy good in his labour. This also I saw, that it was from the hand of God.

Ecclesiastes 3:13—And also that every man should eat and drink, and enjoy the good of all his labour, it is the gift of God.

Finding Wisdom

Proverbs 3:13—Happy is the man that findeth wisdom, and the man that getteth understanding.

Proverbs 3:18—She is a tree of life to them that lay hold upon her: and happy is every one that retaineth her.

Helping Others

Proverbs 14:21—He that despiseth his neighbour sinneth: but he that hath mercy on the poor, happy is he.

Speaking Kind and Gracious Things

Proverbs 15:23—A man hath joy by the answer of his mouth: and a word spoken in due season, how good is it!

Living Honestly

Proverbs 21:15—It is joy to the just to do judgment: but destruction shall be to the workers of iniquity.

Keeping a Tender Heart Toward God

Proverbs 28:14—Happy is the man that feareth alway: but he that hardeneth his heart shall fall into mischief.

Understanding Salvation and Forgiveness

Isaiah 61:10—I will greatly rejoice in the LORD, my soul shall be joyful in my God; for He hath clothed me with the garments of salvation, He hath covered me with the robe of righteousness, as a bridegroom decketh himself with ornaments, and as a bride adorneth herself with her jewels.

Keeping Christ's Commandments

John 13:17—If ye know these things, happy are ye if ye do them.

John 15:11—These things have I spoken unto you, that My joy might remain in you, and that your joy might be full.

Seeing Answered Prayer

John 16:24—Hitherto have ye asked nothing in my name: ask, and ye shall receive, that your joy may be full.

Having a Clear Conscience

Romans 14:22—Hast thou faith? Have it to thyself before God. Happy is he that condemneth not himself in that thing which he alloweth.

A happy heart results from setting one's heart and mind on godly things.

Lesson One: The Secret of a Happy Heart

Answers:

1. salvation
2. Word
3. obey
4. know; do
5. joy might be full

Lesson Two: The Joy of Receiving God's Blessings

Answers:

1. delights; meditates on it
2. fears the Lord
3. His testimonies; God; whole heart
4. her children
5. the Lord
6. in trouble

Lesson Three: The Joy of a Meek and Quiet Spirit

Answers:

1. commandments (testimonies); heart
2. grievous
3. trusts
4. sin; sin
5. gave commandments
6. trusting the Lord

Lesson Four: The Joy of God's Forgiveness

Answers:

1. his sin; ignore it
2. God
3. washes (cleanses/forgives) their sin
4. His salvation
5. sing
6. broken spirit; contrite (humble) heart

Lesson Five: The Joy of Forgiving Others

Answers:
1. angry; pass over it/let it go
2. help
3. defend
4. glad; joy
5. good; pleasant; unity
6. mercy

Lesson Six: The Joy of Christian Womanhood – Part One

Answers:
1. submissive
2. wise
3. the rod; reproof
4. God
5. believes
6. wisdom

Lesson Seven: The Joy of Christian Womanhood – Part Two

Answers:
1. be well with her
2. joyful
3. walk in truth
4. judgment
5. joy

Lesson Eight: The Joy of Overcoming Disappointments

Answers:
1. sorrow
2. it is for her profit
3. the Lord
4. her reward in Heaven is great
5. believes

Lesson Nine: The Joy of Overcoming Impossible Circumstances

Answers:
1. in trouble; glorify
2. endures
3. comfort
4. pain
5. joy

Lesson Ten: The Joy of Understanding Anger

Answers:
1. mouth
2. believes
3. glad
4. joy
5. the ways
6. fear of the Lord
7. sings

Lesson Eleven: The Joy of Conquering Anger

Answers:
1. discretion
2. understanding
3. wrath
4. edify

Lesson Twelve: The Joy of Happy Thoughts

Answers:
1. merry heart
2. thinks
3. lovingkindness
4. meditates on God's goodness
5. thinks on right things

Titus 2 Series

Secrets of a Happy Heart
This study covers topics such as genuine happiness versus false happiness, a happy heart versus an empty heart, a clear conscience versus a guilty conscience, forgiveness versus bitterness, trust versus anger, and contentment versus selfishness and pride.   S. Retail: 14.95

Happily Married
This study covers topics such as love and attraction, one plus one does equal one, submission and leadership, living in a difficult marriage, resolving problems, and a host of other topics such as trust, communication, teamwork, and physical enjoyment.   S. Retail: 14.95

Parenting With Wisdom (formerly *Precept Upon Precept*)
This book addresses key parenting issues such as loving, understanding, disciplining, and motivating children, as well as confronting children who are in rebellion.   S. Retail: 18.95

What to Do When You are Abused by Your Husband
Debi Pryde, Robert Needham
This book offers a biblical perspective of hope and lasting peace, concepts often foreign to abuse situations.   S. Retail: 6.95

Why Am I So Angry?
Written for the counselor and counselee, this book provides a clear definition of anger, a description of the many roots of anger, and a section with personal applications to help conquer anger.   S. Retail: 16.95

Why Am I So Depressed?
Designed to be an all-in-one resource for counselors and counselees, this book is filled with biblical principles and practical applications that will help readers grasp the trustworthy truths that will set them free from the torments of depression.   S. Retail: 11.95

Saved Without a Doubt
This booklet clarifies in layman terms the key truths concerning salvation and the assurance of salvation.   S. Retail: 1.95

Guiding Principles for the Biblical Counselor
This is a collection of lecture notes, worksheets, biblical counseling lessons, and topical Bible studies for use in counseling and discipleship. The material in this toolbook will assist counselors with a sincere desire to hone their application of Scripture to life's problems. This study of biblical counseling principles, methodology, and theological considerations will provide a basis for continued study and will provoke believers to become excited about the power God's Word has to change lives and to solve problems.   S. Retail: 11.95

Companion Seminar CD's for Guiding Principles
Join the author as she teaches through each chapter during a seminar at Ironwood. This 20 CD set comes in a zipper case for durability.   S. Retail: $70.00

TO ORDER: 760.257.3503
WWW.IRONWOOD.ORG

LESSON ONE

The Secret of a Happy Heart

LESSON TWO

The Joy of Receiving God's Blessings

LESSON THREE

The Joy of a Meek and Quiet Spirit

LESSON FOUR

The Joy of God's Forgiveness

LESSON FIVE

The Joy of Forgiving Others

LESSON SIX

The Joy of Christian Womanhood - Part One

LESSON SEVEN

The Joy of Christian Womanhood - Part Two

LESSON EIGHT

The Joy of Overcoming Disappointments

Blessed be the Lord, who daily loadeth us with benefits, even the God of our salvation.
Psalm 68:19

And all these blessings shall come on thee, and overtake thee, if thou shalt hearken unto the voice of the LORD thy God.
Deuteronomy 28:2

Secrets of a Happy Heart - Memory Verses

Favor is deceitful, and beauty is vain: but a woman that feareth the LORD, she shall be praised.
Proverbs 31:30

The secret of the LORD is with them that fear Him.
Psalm 25:14a

Secrets of a Happy Heart - Memory Verses

He that covereth his sins shall not prosper: but whoso confesseth and forsaketh them shall have mercy. Happy is the man that feareth always: but he that hardeneth his heart shall fall into mischief.
Proverbs 28:13-14

If we confess our sins, He is faithful and just to forgive us our sins and to cleanse us from all unrighteousness. If we say that we have not sinned, we make Him a liar, and His Word is not in us.
1 John 1:9-10

Secrets of a Happy Heart - Memory Verses

But let it be the hidden man of the heart, in that which is not corruptible, even the ornament of a meek and quiet spirit, which is in the sight of God of great price.
1 Peter 3:4

But He giveth more grace. Wherefore He saith, God resisteth the proud, but giveth grace unto the humble.
James 4:6

Secrets of a Happy Heart - Memory Verses

Blessed are they that keep His testimonies, and that seek Him with the whole heart.
Psalm 119:2

Thy testimonies have I taken as heritage forever, for they are the rejoicing of my heart.
Psalm 119:111

Secrets of a Happy Heart - Memory Verses

And be ye kind one to another, tenderhearted, forgiving one another, even as God for Christ's sake hath forgiven you.
Ephesians 4:32

The discretion of a man deferreth his anger; and it is his glory to pass over a transgression.
Proverbs 19:11

Secrets of a Happy Heart - Memory Verses

Casting all your care upon Him: for He careth for you.
1 Peter 5:7

My soul, wait thou only upon God; for my expectation is from Him. He only is my rock and my salvation; He is my defense; I shall not be moved.
Psalm 62:5-6

Secrets of a Happy Heart - Memory Verses

Strength and honor are her clothing; and she shall rejoice in time to come.
Proverbs 31:25

Give her of the fruit of her hands; and let her own works praise her in the gates.
Proverbs 31:31

Secrets of a Happy Heart - Memory Verses

LESSON NINE

The Joy of Overcoming Impossible Circumstances

LESSON TEN

The Joy of Understanding Anger

LESSON ELEVEN

The Joy of Conquering Anger

LESSON TWELVE

The Joy of Happy Thoughts

APPENDIX

Things That God Says Make Us Happy

SUMMARY VERSES

Principle: Happiness is a gift from God

THEME VERSES

Titus 2 Bible Study Series

THEME VERSES

Titus 2 Bible Study Series

To comfort all that mourn, to appoint unto them that mourn in Zion, to give unto them beauty for ashes, the oil of joy for mourning, the garment of praise for the spirit of heaviness; that they might be called trees of righteousness, the planting of the LORD, that He might be glorified.
Isaiah 61:2b-3

My flesh and my heart faileth: but God is the strength of my heart, and my portion forever.
Psalm 73:26

Secrets of a Happy Heart - Memory Verses

Thou shalt not hate thy brother in thine heart: thou shalt in any wise rebuke thy neighbor, and not suffer sin upon him. Thou shalt not avenge, nor bear any grudge against the children of thy people, but thou shalt love thy neighbor as thyself: I am the LORD.
Leviticus 19:17-18

Wherefore, my beloved brethren, let every man be swift to hear, slow to speak, slow to wrath: for the wrath of man worketh not the righteousness of God.
James 1:19-20

Secrets of a Happy Heart - Memory Verses

A stone is heavy, and the sand weighty; but a fool's wrath is heavier than them both.
Proverbs 27:3

Be not hasty in the spirit to be angry; for anger resteth in the bosom of fools.
Ecclesiastes 7:9

Secrets of a Happy Heart - Memory Verses

In the multitude of my thoughts within me, Thy comforts delight my soul.
Psalm 94:19

Finally, brethren, whatsoever things are true, whatsoever things are honest, whatsoever things are just, whatsoever things are pure, whatsoever things are lovely, whatsoever things are of good report; if there be anyvirtue, and if there be any praise, think on these things.
Philippians 4:8

Secrets of a Happy Heart - Memory Verses

Every man also to whom God hath given riches and wealth, and hath given him power to eat thereof, and to take his portion, and to rejoice in his labour; this is the gift of God. For he shall not much remember the days of his life; because God answereth him in the joy of his heart.
Ecclesiastes 5:19-20

Secrets of a Happy Heart - Memory Verses

This book of the law shall not depart out of thy mouth; but thou shalt meditate therein day and night, that thou mayest observe to do according to all that is written therein: for then thou shalt make thy way prosperous, and then thou shalt have good success.
Joshua 1:8

And these things write we unto you, that your joy may be full.
1 John 1:4

Secrets of a Happy Heart - Memory Verses

Young men likewise exhort to be sober minded. In all things showing thyself a pattern of good works: in doctrine *showing* uncorruptness, gravity, sincerity, sound speech, that cannot be condemned; that he that is of the contrary part may be ashamed, having no evil thing to say of you.
Titus 2:6-8

Secrets of a Happy Heart - Memory Verses

That they may teach the young women to be sober, to love their husbands, to love their children, to be discreet, chaste, keepers at home, good, obedient to their own husbands, that the word of God be not blasphemed.
Titus 2:4-5

Secrets of a Happy Heart - Memory Verses